FORGOTTEN JOURNEY

FORGOTTEN JOURNEY

Every Man's Dream, Every Wife's Nightmare

By Nan Prodan

To my patient beta readers, who kept me going while I was stranded on an island off Mexico.

To my final beta reader, my sister-in-law, whom I reconnected with on social media after forty years. Thank you for asking all the right questions. And to Jim, the Best captain in the world.

Contents

CHAPTER ONE

Adventure

I t might not be good news, but maybe it would be good enough to give her a fighting chance. Before Meg made her decision to go ahead with the test, she considered her mental ability to deal with the outcome. She read about the three types of genes they would be checking for. The *ApoE3* gene removed plaque from the brain reasonably well; those persons didn't have an increased or decreased risk of developing the disease. The *ApoE2* gene also removed plaque from the brain, and those persons had a reduced risk of development—the good results and what she hoped for. The *ApoE4* gene, the bad one, increased the chances of development by 50 percent. Given both Tom's and Meg's mothers' diagnoses, when Meg took the smear from the inside of her cheek, she fulfilled an obligatory duty due to each one of them. Both had passed with their memories stolen. The results would be waiting for her at the end of their trip.

From her first-class seat, Meg Trumbo saw a familiar view of Overseas Highway snaking through the multihued shallow blue water. To Meg, not widely traveled, the Florida Keys were the prettiest place on earth. The Keys were 120 miles long, and at one point, she saw all of the seventeen hundred islands as the plane flew from east to west. Midway, Meg saw a boat passing through Moser Channel, a deep water cut through the Seven Mile Bridge to the Gulf of Mexico.

"They must be going to Naples," she thought to herself. She and Tom had done it many times.

At the end of the highway, one could see the city of Key West. A city of events all year long, made famous by Hemingway's time there in the thirties before he moved on to Cuba. The only thing more striking than the overhead view of a highway surrounded by water would be to fly into the United States' southernmost point at sunset. The flight came in over Mallory Dock, where a gathering of jugglers and mimes, fire-eaters and tightrope walkers, and musicians and vendors set up before crowds celebrating the end of yet another beautiful day in paradise.

With her dog on her lap, Meg reviewed the notes she had made on her phone, checking things off her list. The destination was new for them. Tom had planned for three years. He had talked about it with captains he knew and compared notes. He had purchased a chart for his GPS, a global positioning system. It detailed the route, and he studied it. A long trip—not as long as the trip they'd taken to Sint Maarten but the longest without stopping. Meg had anxiety. They had done a great deal of cruising, been many places. This time they had to leave Key West in the wee morning hours to arrive at their destination before sundown. The thought of going out in water thousands of feet deep in the dark terrified her. The unknown kept her up at night and gave her nightmares.

Meg told herself, "Tom is an experienced captain. He doesn't take chances." Still, Meg struggled with it.

What if something happened to one of them, out there all alone?

They had traveled hundreds of miles in open water in the Caribbean, the two of them and the dog. There had been no problems. The blackness was what Meg feared. She worried about unseen floating wreckage in the water, boats with no lights in their path, loss of power, or an onboard fire. And her mind had five more things on its list. All the things that would be a dilemma in the daylight would be a tragedy in the dark. Normally, she would already be with him there in Key West. They would drive the boat down and wait for a weather window. But her test kept her back. And he wasn't pleased.

After their thirty years of marriage, their time in business together, raising their daughter in a cold climate, and never having been boaters before, Tom's pursuit of adventure brought excitement to Meg's life. Meg knew if she had been the dominant force in the relationship, it would have never occurred. While Tom possessed the courage and desire to do more things, he only needed to open the door for Meg, and she would step in.

For some couples this may not have been possible to leave their roots and move on to a different part of the country, away from friends and family to pursue a dream. But they were a team. They depended upon each other, and it worked. They shopped together. They decorated their home together. They ran the boat together. They cooked gourmet meals together. There wasn't much that Tom and Meg Trumbo didn't do together.

Meg loved the silence of Tom's nature. While she had to wait many times for him to come forward with his innermost thoughts and feelings, he never disappointed her. He loved her from their beginning. Would she hear it often from his lips? No, probably not. But actions, she knew, always spoke loudly.

When they planned the trip, more to satisfy Meg, they had discussed hiring a captain to go along with them. Last they talked, Tom had hired a captain in Key West who had made the trip many times before and would go with them. They'd fly him back to Key West the next day.

On her plane's approach to the Key West airport, the captain apologized for a delay in landing. Due to traffic on the runway, he circled, and they flew out over the Dry Tortugas. Other passengers without a window seat stood up and leaned in to get a view of the sanctuary for fish and wildlife. Fort Jefferson, an old Civil War prison, had become a popular destination for divers and campers and those healthy enough to maneuver the climb to the top. The view from the fort made it worth the hike. Far off the left wing of Silver Airlines flight 111, two F/A 18 Super Hornet jets from the US Naval Air Station blasted by and vibrated her window before making a full circle to the left and vanishing in the sky. Everyone on board applauded.

"Thank you, folks," the captain announced. "Glad you liked the show."

Another ten minutes and the tower called them in. They were on the ground in ten more. Meg got an Uber to take her the fifteen-minute ride to the marina. She could see their boat, *Tori's Seacret*, tied up at the end of the dock by the big fishing boats. It had the longest outriggers on the dock. When Meg got there, Tom wasn't on the boat. He'd left her a note.

At lunchtime, she knew where he'd be. The best spot in town for a hot dog and fries.

Meg walked the Key West dock, anxious to see Tom. The little white dog trotted next to her. Bitti pulled on her leash to sniff the pea rock next to the boardwalk. It was the place where the other dogs peed, and she wanted to pee there too. They went by the stinky fishing boats and the huddled crowds of tourists out to see the morning's catch. The mates stuck the cold bodies of the fish on the nails over the cleaning tables. On the sign over each table were the names of the boats. There were *Sea Dog*, *Sir Reel*, *Finchaser*, *Deep Throat*, and ten more. All for charter every day at the bight. Sweaty fishermen cleaned the fresh fish, one by one, and tossed the carcasses to the giant tarpon rolling below in the water. Brown pelicans coasted in and snapped up their share.

Ahead of her, the captain Tom had hired leaned with his knee bent and his foot on the bricks and mortar of Schooner Warf Bar. Skinny Jack, so he was called, saw Meg heading his way. She knew of him, and he recognized her by her T-shirt, and he sheepishly grinned at Meg. His blond handlebar mustache ridden with gray framed his mouth, and his front and center gold tooth glistened when he smiled.

"I know," he half apologized, cocking his head. "I am supposed to keep off the whiskey for the trip, but the pressure got to me. I promise I'll be ready to go tomorrow."

Meg wouldn't respond to him, dare she chase him off. After all the discussion she and Tom had over hiring him, she was disappointed. Tom took offense to her questioning his expertise. In fact, Tom didn't like to be questioned at all. He didn't understand her fear. Meg made a sharp right turn in front of Skinny Jack into Schooner's, where her husband sat at the bar drinking a bottle of Key West Ale. He had a basket of fries and a foot-long hot dog. When Tom saw her come through the door, he smiled at the sight of her, but the look on her face was telltale, as always. It told him what she was thinking, and his wife was not happy.

A guy on the stage played "Margaritaville," and the crowd shouted out the words when a familiar refrain came along. The same guy every afternoon and the same patrons at the bar. Meg plopped onto a barstool, and Bitti curled up on the floor made of rocks.

"Did you see your captain out there?" Meg sarcastically tossed her words at him. "He can't even be sober at noon. Or at least hide it. There must have been others to choose from, Tom."

He threw her words right back at her. "He's a character. He'll be ready to go tomorrow. They make these trips all the time. It's part of his prep. Give the guy a break, will you? Remember, a real captain was your idea."

Meg had made her point, and to argue would be moot, but she needed to squeeze in one more wisecrack remark. "So, the captain is a drunk. Who cares if we all die at sea?" Then she motioned to the bartender and ordered a beer in a cold frosty mug. The only way Meg thought one should drink a beer. After half-gone, Meg sang along with the rest of the crowd, swaying with the music on the stool next to Tom. They were in Key West, Florida, the launching pad for sport fishers heading to Mexico.

Later, Meg lay like a stiff in their bed, straining to stop her brain from overthinking. Who knew when she'd sleep again? Every time Meg closed her eyes, she caught herself at it again, worrying about the trip only a few hours away. After their years together, Meg still didn't have a list to put in her bucket. She wasn't about adventure. She lived her life checking things off Tom's list. But this time, whether it was her age or the fear that sooner or later tragedy would find them, she had put her foot down and said no. But Tom found a way to pick it up. He wanted to go. This trip was a new quest of accomplishment in life for him. It was what the big sport fishers did. And he wanted to do that too. For Meg, it was her need to stand by him as she always had. Did she always agree? Was she always silent and submissive?

At 1:50 a.m., Meg fell into a deep sleep. Ten minutes later, the theme song from *Rocky* on her iPhone rudely jolted her awake. Tom was still asleep. She gave him a nudge.

"I am taking Bitti now."

Four hundred miles and fourteen hours, and there would be no stopping for Bitti. Meg scoured the dimly lit dock, searching for a sign of Skinny Jack. Except for her and Bitti, no one else was around.

Will this guy show? She halfheartedly wondered.

After Bitti did all she could do, Meg and Bitti zigzagged along the half-mile wooden dock to the boat. The one-hundred-slip marina was packed, but no one was awake. A watchdog howled on a tugboat motoring out when she and Bitti hurried by. *Tori's Seacret*'s fifteen hundred horsepower MTU engines roared. The running lights were on, and Tom had removed most of the dock lines from the cleats.

"Come on," he called to her. "It's time to go. It looks like Jack's not coming. I guess we don't want him to." His voice apologized.

Meg got on and locked the dog in the salon. Meg asked herself. When did Tom find out Jack wasn't coming? Was this now her fault? Because of how she acted at the bar yesterday when she saw Jack? Not a good way to start off the trip. But the spine-chilling chant of the "Conquest of Paradise" poured from their speakers and echoed throughout the seaport filling Tom's soul with fearless passion. He stood tall at the helm. As always first mate, Meg scathed the side of the monster, and once up to the bow, she lifted the starboard and port lines off splintered wood pilings. In her hurry she forgot her gloves and a piece stuck into her thumb. No time now. Meg crouched on the bow to wrap and tie the lines for storage in the anchor locker. When Tom saw Meg safely off the bow and into the cockpit, he put the engines in forward, and *Tori's Seacret* crept out of her slip. Tom maneuvered the tight left turn out of the marina. Skinny Jack stood back in the shadows on the bight and snapped a photo of *Tori's Seacret* as she disappeared from sight. He tossed the empty bottle of Old Crow into the bight and went home to bed.

The wide waterway was well marked. The red beacon glowed on their left. The green guided them on their right. The clear shallow water of the rocky reef was all around them. Tom's route on the GPS showed them the way. The lights from the monitors were the only lights in the flybridge. *Tori's Seacret* followed the course. Meg turned and watched the fading lights of Key West. Estimated time of arrival: 5:00 p.m., Isla Mujeres, "Woman Island," off the coast of the Yucatán.

Three hours and ninety miles south of Key West, the pitch dark of the night courted *Tori's Seacret* in the deepest waters of the Gulf Stream. Up in the flybridge, Tom's medium frame sat comfortably in the captain's chair. His bare feet were propped up on the helm. In the mate's chair to the left of him, Meg's legs dangled a foot from the deck, and Bitti rode on her lap. Meg glanced behind them, did a double take, and pointed.

"Oh my God! Tom."

The crimson glow on the horizon previewed the dawning of the new day in Key West. Each minute that passed, it became more intense. Within moments, the rising sun gained on them, and a speck of light peeked out. A white star rising made yellow, then red orange, by the atmosphere scattered colors all over the water. The sky and the water blended together until Tom and Meg couldn't distinguish one from the other. The red fireball exploded before their eyes, and it challenged any sunset they had seen in their lives. Meg videoed the breathtaking panorama.

Purple and pale pink hues spread over the water, showcasing three bottlenose dolphins on the surface. They dove in *Tori's Seacret*'s wake and swirled up in the air and gave the crew a private show. Then just like they'd appeared, the dolphins were gone. Tom's eyes smiled at Meg's, and her eyes smiled back. A forgiveness moment they needed between them. Meg's eyes watered, and she reached to touch him.

Tom and Meg were high on a drug called exhilaration. They'd left in the dark from Key West. All their planning paid off—no, his planning. She'd misjudged, too tough on him; they didn't need a captain after all.

CHAPTER TWO
Red Sky at Night

An ancient rhyme referenced in the New Testament never came to mind: red sky at night, sailors' delight; red sky at morning, sailors take warning. *Tori's Seacret* skimmed the top of the flat water at thirty miles an hour. If a swordfish or blue marlin were swimming by, Tom and Meg would have seen it. A rooster tail of water from the propulsion of the engines shot up like a fountain. Tom wanted to increase the speed, but this was not necessary. *Tori's Seacret* gave them a ride with not a bump or a splash, and they were enjoying every minute of it.

At first, brewing storm clouds couldn't be seen. They began small and disconnected then blossomed out and joined together and surrounded the boat. A roll of smoky black clouds stealthily moved in. Tom could slow up and wait it out, but experience told him that, eventually, it would reach them. Turning back was not an option. They could hear the thunder, but the lightning hid from them.

The design of an outrigger challenged lightning. Aluminum pieces of metal sticking up high in the sky scream out in a storm, "Here I am; come get me." A direct strike would disable the boat's steering, radio, and GPS systems. Touching the steering wheel or any metal in the flybridge, a soul could get a jolt or be tossed off in the water. Or worse, the vessel could explode in a ball of fire. Tom adjusted the radar to expand its scope to see how many miles they would travel before the rain would hit them. Meg could smell it. The cross icon representing *Tori's Seacret* on the radar screen moved along like an object in a video game. The interference splotched on the screen ahead of them showed rain, and it went on for ten miles. Their wait for the boat and the storm to meet up was a nail-biter. Twice Tom pulled her fingers from her mouth. He whistled a tune. Meg knew he did it to relieve the tension. Meg was thankful it was Tom's business card that read *Captain*.

The wind came first. It hit the port side of the boat and grabbed the bow, moving it over. It caused a vibration through the lines on the outriggers, and the orifices wailed. Tom reacted and placed both hands on the wheel and disengaged the autopilot. The rain came next. It moved at them off the port side. Huge drops sounding like bullets pelleted the hardtop. It was louder than the engines. The droplets of rain became sheets that swept the enclosure on the flybridge. There were no wipers to move the rain aside. The rumbling of the thunder came closer, and now each time a flash enlightened the helm, they held their breath for the next one.

Nature had thrown a white bedsheet over the boat, and Tom had to control the panic in his gut. He backed off the throttles to reduce his speed to eight miles an hour. The waves splashed over the hardtop and into the helm through the small screened openings and soaked them. Meg and Bitti nestled close together while Meg held on, but the wind gusts became so strong the two of them were rocked side to side. Meg's head jogged back and forth, and she knew the dull pain in her neck would ache the following day. The water's deep, dark blue changed to frothy white, whipped up by the action of the wind and the waves. The wind became an artist who took his finger and added a blob of white paint to his original blue canvas, stroking up and down in spikes and back and forth in circles. It became a sea of milk of magnesia.

Whispering under her breath, Meg shook her head. "Never, ever, again."

Tom either didn't hear or chose not to comment. He stood rigid at the helm and kept the boat on course. One after another, waves splashed into the enclosure and soaked them again and again. They shivered. Meg's nipples stood up in her T-shirt. Along with the salty seawater, pieces of foul-smelling sargassum weed slapped their cheeks. It was a type of seaweed that floated in ocean currents. Shrimp, crab, worms, squid, and even tiny sea turtles made their life there. Bubbling schools of baitfish fed on them while bonito chased them out of the water. The thousand-pound marlin watched from the deep, waiting to strike.

Tom's and Meg's eyeglasses were caked with salt, and while the water splashed in, there was no resolving it. Tom hated the storm as much as he loved the calm. The calm days were the only thing that kept him coming back for more. Like the weekend golfer's hole in one kept him playing the following Saturday.

That early morning, Tom Trumbo had left Key West feeling good. They'd seen the awe-inspiring sunrise, the colors on the water, and the playful dolphins and enjoyed the calm ride. Meg didn't know what Tom was thinking, but she wanted to be someplace else. Two of the three GPS systems were not responding. Either the primary circuit had blown or the breakers inside the helm compartment had popped. Tom was doing the navigation in zero visibility, while Meg had her eyes glued in front of her, holding her breath, hoping their blindness didn't mask a calamity at sea.

Tom expelled a sigh of relief when a small patch of blue appeared through the clouds ahead of them. He rechecked his radar screen, and the worst was behind them. Bitti was belted into her hot-pink life preserver. She shivered. A tongue too swollen for her tiny mouth caused saliva to drain on the deck beneath her. The rain began to let up, and Meg got out a few dry towels from under the seat. She splashed fresh water on Bitti's mouth and then on her and Tom's glasses. She wrapped one towel snugly around Bitti to dry her off and make her feel more secure. The sea was a crummy, gritty feeling all over them. The ocean water still had whitecaps, but the waves were getting smaller, and the distance between them was widening. It had been a rough few hours for all aboard *Tori's Seacret*.

They couldn't see land. Tom leaned back in his chair and ran his hands through his wet, tousled hair. He descended the ladder to the cabin to use the head. It had been a while. He checked the circuit breakers on the panel. They were active. Meg stood at the helm with a keen eye on the compass to keep the boat on the proper heading. He slowed their speed a little more so they could talk without screaming. They shared a few moments of peace, and Meg went down below and filled a soft cooler bag with sandwiches, potato chips, and bottles of water for all three of them. She put a handful of kibble in her pocket.

Meg climbed the ladder carefully. The salt-covered rails and steps were slick, and she searched for a clean area to grab as she moved up each rung. A broken bone would not be good. Meg began divvying up lunch on a spot in front of the steering wheel as Tom stared with interest off to the east. His eyebrows narrowed, bringing up a questioning frown. Far off in the distance, amid a flat sea, a dark wall of water churned. Unexpected by Meg, Tom turned the wheel. Lunch fell onto the deck, and the bottles of water tumbled off the bridge and hurtled into the cockpit.

"What are you doing?"

Tom frowned at her. He hated being questioned.

Meg's mind was sorry, but then she did it again, the next time louder. "Are we turning around?"

Tom turned again, this time to the right to correct his course. He turned so sharply and abruptly that Meg swung in the opposite direction and fell onto the bench seat. Bitti was tied to the flybridge rail. The turn pulled the dog forward and then back and she squealed when it gave her body a strong jerk. Her water spilled, and a wave hit the enclosure again. It splashed inside the flybridge and drizzled on them. The dog licked the saltwater taste from her mouth, and Meg wiped the salt from her glasses again. Eyes front and center, Meg viewed a phenomenon few had ever witnessed and one she would never forget.

Rogue waves were rare, and although Tom had never experienced one, others had warned about them. Seamen reported rogue waves that possessed the power to sink ocean-going vessels. A rogue wave had been reported at a wave height of sixty feet while the surface winds were only at fifteen knots. It was their unpredictability that made them so hazardous.

Sensing danger, Bitti's body trembled from the panting. Her eyes bugged, and her ears rested flat on the sides of her head. The dread built in Meg's body. Snowballing vibrations traveled up and down her spine, and the wave became broader, higher, and closer. It brought to mind pictures she had seen of tsunami waves in Thailand that pushed everything in their path on the land out of their way. While tsunami waves moved through the water, rogue waves sat on top. There was no time for planning. Meg untied Bitti from the rail.

Tom did the only thing he knew to do, steering directly into the wave as *Tori's Seacret* began her climb to the crest. Tom pushed the throttles all the way forward, hoping the engines had enough muscle to conquer the briny beast. Up, up, up, until her stern stood squarely perpendicular to the sea level below them. *Tori's Seacret*, like a roller coaster, waited to go up the track, and then take the plunge. The ride down the other side would give Tom and Meg the sinking feeling in their stomachs they remembered from childhood. The feeling would have been enough to be their best hope.

When *Tori's Seacret* met the crest, the fear in Tom's gut screamed out at him. His skill had betrayed him. He closed his eyes and instinctively pushed the throttles more, but there was no more.

"Damn you, damn you, damn you, Tom Trumbo," he screamed.

Meg's head jerked and her knees buckled when her feet slipped from under her. She held Bitti close to her ribs and gripped the railing. Donning their life vests, the three of them were not prepared for what fate had planned for them. *Tori's Seacret* was flipping over.

At last look, Meg saw dripping auburn ringlets framing Tom's face. His knuckles were white. His dark red-brown skin contrasted his eyes, which stood out like turquoise gems. They flashed like the eyes of a conqueror on the cover of a romance novel. Tom met fear and the rogue wave all at once. Meg had never seen her husband like that before. That memory of Tom Trumbo became etched in her mind.

CHAPTER THREE

Mea Culpa, Mea Culpa, Mea Culpa

Then it was over. No telling how much time had gone by before Meg came to. The water became peaceful. Bitti was gone. Meg didn't remember Tom pulling back on the throttles after the wave, but the boat moved at idle, and a person was speaking, a woman broadcasting over the radio—the US Coast Guard on channel sixteen. Meg grabbed the receiver and rambled a message.

"Mayday, Mayday, Mayday! This is *Tori's Seacret*." She repeated, "Mayday, Mayday, Mayday! Sport fisher *Tori's Seacret* off the coast of Cuba." Then she waited. Nothing.

Meg judged the boat's location from the position of the sun. She continued to send her message at regular intervals. The woman on the coast guard channel added an alert to nearby mariners that a vessel had been reported missing. It had never arrived at its destination. The name of the boat was *Tori's Seacret*.

"We're here." Did Meg hear Tom say this? But the woman speaking on the radio still didn't respond.

Meg's eyes squinted, and her mind questioned what she believed Tom had said to her. "What is the extent of the damages?" Words Tom would say to mechanics at home echoed over and over in her head. Her forehead was tender when she put her hand on it to pull her hair off her face. Climbing down to the cockpit, Meg's legs wobbled, and her head spun like a top. To stabilize herself, Meg grabbed the wood rail when she opened the door of the boat. The electrical panel was ajar, and all the switches were on. In the galley, the refrigerators were at temperature, and freezers were making ice. Everything was good.

Next, she went to check their cabin. Pillows were tossed on the floor. She opened the large mirrored closet. At the bottom were their liquor and wine inventories. Nothing there had moved.

Queasiness overcame her and took her to bed. If she was seasick, staying in the cabin was not a remedy. The passage of time became confusing. Her watch had stopped at 10:20 p.m. She didn't know if it was morning or afternoon. Was that yesterday or the day before? Moving out to the open air, Meg felt better. She couldn't see Tom at the helm. Maybe he was below it fixing the GPS breakers. But when Meg opened the door beneath the helm, it was empty.

With an unstable mental state, Meg had to struggle to keep her thinking in line with her mission. If she had one, she didn't know what it was. Other times Tom had told her if they kept their speed at idle, they could go a long way on the maybe fifteen hundred gallons of fuel remaining in the tanks. She had learned that and other things from him, and now she needed to remember all of them to survive.

She climbed up and down again to the cockpit to lug up bottles of water. Dehydration could set in quickly. Actually, it already had. It happened to Tom a lot. Once it took over his body, it would be too late. The brain would shrink in the skull. His eyes would blur, and he'd get headaches from the loss of potassium. Dehydration further caused muscle fatigue and cramping. He'd hold up his hands, and they would be frozen and rendered useless from the lack of strength and the pain. He couldn't hold on to the wheel. Afterward, there would be dizziness, delirium, and unconsciousness. With her medical training, Meg recognized the symptoms and knew the remedy. Meg recalled asking him to drink water and put a bottle out for him, but after a while, in the cup holder, it was still there unopened. Could it have been yesterday? Was it for Tom, or was it for Meg?

If she saw her pallid skin and the blood dried on her scalp, she'd know it was she who was feeling these things. Exhaustion told her to lie down. This time she lay in the flybridge. Sleep came, then a dream. In the fantasy, she hooked bait on three fishing rods. They were whoppers with large preset hooks that slipped right on. She put one rod in the rocket launcher in the center on the stern, one on the port-side outrigger, and one on the starboard-side rigger. She released the line on the center rod and used the two outriggers to hold the port and starboard lines away from the boat. When the bait hit the water, bam! The lines whizzed out. Fish on. Fish on. Fish on.

One hit. Two hits. Three hits. "Oh my gosh!" Meg screamed.

Even though Meg had never told Tom, when they fished in the past, she'd always prayed for no fish. But her prayers never worked. The episode remained the same. He drove the boat, and she struggled to bring in the lines before they became a tangled bird's nest. The fish feeding on the baits to the port and starboard were giant tuna. They usually dove deep. The line on the center pole lay slack in the water. Meg believed she saw a blue marlin, but they must have missed it. Meg's hand spun the reel as fast as it could, but she moved in slow motion. Meg couldn't understand why, but dreams did that to her. The marlin was still on the line deep, and it was swimming up fast. Meg had to collect all of the slack quickly to keep control of the fish. She reeled, dipping in forward and then pulling up and back on the fish, hoping to tire it out.

Like always, Tom coached her, "Pull up, reel down. Pull up, reel down. Pull up, reel down. Faster, reel faster." He screamed at her, almost cruelly. He hated to lose.

Meg continued as long as she could and hoped she might get a glimpse of it. But then the big fish began pulling away from the boat again, and she let the line spin off the reel with the fish. She was a slight woman; her right wrist bent, cramped in horrible pain. Her left hand and arm were holding the weight of the rod against her body, but she needed the fighting belt. Tom came down from the flybridge and put the belt on her hips and the end of the rod in the cup of the belt.

He slapped her on her tush and said, "Go, get um, Meg!"

But even with the belt, she didn't know how much longer she could do it. Bam! There it went again.! Meg watched as the blue marlin exploded out of the water like a rocket. She tightened the reel until the line became taut, and the fish's tail walked on water like the bronze statue on their galley counter. She had a more magnificent fish than either of them had ever seen. And Meg had caught it.

Now there were sharks in the water. The tuna on the port line lay taut without much movement, so Meg took a knife and cut it loose. The tuna on the starboard side was struggling to survive, and Meg cut him loose also, hoping it would draw the sharks away from the marlin. To bring it to the boat to declare it a legal catch was Meg's goal. Her prize thrashed, but it finally gave in, as if it knew the boat was where it needed to come to get free. Meg carefully removed the hook from the marlin's open gnawing mouth, and its glassy eye gave her a wink before diving away from the boat. Meg's catch escaped the fate of the fish in *The Old Man and the Sea*, and it made her proud.

Flocks of birds circled the boat. Their screams woke Meg from her dream, and she leaned over the side and searched the water for her marlin. She thought about the marlin Tom had caught, but he'd never gotten one as mighty as hers.

A sweet little thumb-sized yellow-breasted Cuban vireo landed in the cockpit to hitch a ride. Meg had seen migratory vireos in her backyard trees singing cheerful melodies. They often flew ninety miles to the Florida Keys from Cuba seeking love. Tom said, and she knew it to be true, that birds mated for life, but like Meg, this bird huddled without hers. Meg and the bird had something in common. She filled a container with fresh water and carried it to the stole away, but the bird had taken flight. Meg wondered if the bird's eye had seen the little dog in the water.

"At least the bird knew the way," Meg said longingly.

Meg began to physically feel better. The water worked wonders and fed her brain, and a sandwich made her feel human again. A sunset was nearing the horizon. Meg went and made drinks, a scotch and soda for her, a gin for him.

Meg watched the sunset alone. Each sip of her drink sat on her tongue before she let it slide into her belly. When she'd drunk half, she left it behind and climbed up to the tuna tower. The tower rose eight feet above the flybridge. Meg climbed the narrow aluminum ladder that became narrower as it reached the top. She crawled under its rail to access the upper helm.

Captains and mates went up there to spot the game fish. There were so many different colors of the water and the currents that cut through it. It resembled little calm rivers winding in and out, taking the sargassum weed and other minuscule debris in the direction it flowed.

Meg would only go up to the tower after a drink. It gave her the courage to make the climb. Meg had warned Tom that one of them would fall from there one day. Meg had a 360-degree view. She squinted, but the sun sat low in the sky and without sunglasses, she was blinded. Glancing at her chafed hands and her wedding band—which needed polishing—Meg saw her skin more bronze than she had ever seen it before. Tom was always the one with the tan. A cool breeze kicked up, blowing her hair back. Checking the horizon one last time before dismounting the tower, Meg caught sight of a boat. She called to Tom.

"I see a boat; we need to head toward the sun." But nothing happened. Meg took control in the upper helm, and *Tori's Seacret* began a full slow turn. Behind them, the two outriggers dangled broken in the path of her wake.

In thirty more minutes, it was dark. A bazillion stars crowded Meg's view. She wondered if it was the Milky Way. Stargazing in the pitch black of night was a no-brainer when there were no lights to steal the wonder of it all. Meg put the helm on autopilot and carefully lugged a cushion up to the bow. If Meg had lost her grip, *Tori's Seacret* would have gone on without her. Pirates could have boarded and stripped her for parts, or she would have ended up on a shallow reef. Eventually, someone would have found the remnants of *Tori's Seacret*, but if Meg went overboard, there would have been no one to tell her story.

If he were on the bow with her, they could glide along and enjoy the night and the stars. Between the liquor, dehydration, and the bump on her head, Meg's thoughts made no sense.

"It's romantic," Meg thought. Tom and Meg did *it* many times, *screwed*, did *the big nasty*. Made love on the bow of the boat, butt naked, or dropped an anchor in the deserted shallow waters of South Caicos. Snorkeled in their birthday suits, as they followed hundreds of little conch feet tracks in the sand with their shells dragging behind.

"Who has ever done these things?" Meg counted herself as blessed.

Meg scanned the water. Lights flickered in the dark. How far off were they, if they were so visible? Meg's eye caught sight of a shooting star, and she stretched her neck to follow it, showering across the sky. It came so near, she reached out to touch it, and when she did, she closed her eyes and made a wish. If a search plane were flying above her, it would have seen *Tori's Seacret's* running lights, with Meg Trumbo laid out on the bow, making a broad circle, around and around and around.

Meg slept very soundly. Jerking as she woke up, Meg found herself still on the bow. The salt made her itchy. Crusty sleep dried in the corners of her eyes and bled into the bags that age had given her. Six in the morning, and there to the east was an old friend. Another day began with a glow of orange that had become a daily companion.

If Meg saw herself in a mirror, she'd be alarmed, but her head was clear. She checked the level of the fuel gauges. *Tori's Seacret* had burned a little more than five hundred gallons. Doing the math, she calculated she had been out there for three days. She had a visual of losing her grip and tumbling off the boat. Thankfully, the tuna door had unlocked and was flapping open; otherwise, there would have been no hope of getting on board. Meg remembered it as more than a challenge to bring her body up onto the boat. She wasn't young anymore and didn't have Tom's strength. She scraped her knees as she kicked her feet to propel herself out of the water on her stomach into the cockpit. Hoisting her butt in couldn't have been a pretty sight, but who was watching? It flashed in Meg's mind that Tom had not been in the boat after they hit the wave. He hadn't sent a message on the radio. Tom didn't answer or join her on the bow. Tom didn't drive or try to remedy the GPS breakers, and they didn't talk about the storm or the wave or the little dog. It had been just Meg on *Tori's Seacret* all along. Her mind, could it be slipping? She said to herself, "No. I am injured. I am stressed."

Meg's dishwater-blond hair was matted red from oozing blood. Using the shower hose in the cockpit, she began rinsing it repeatedly. The warm water was soothing, but the wound bled again. Head wounds did that, and she knew it. After wadding up the gauze to make a bandage, Meg tied it to her head like a headband. She didn't know how she'd gotten the injury, but Meg recalled seeing the flickering lights in the night—which night, she didn't know.

Different theories entered her mind. Tom and Bitti were together and washed overboard, maybe rescued or stranded on an island. She asked herself. Were they playing with a volleyball named Wilson, waiting for help? Her theories were stupid. But those were the kinds of crazy ideas going on in her head. It was as if someone took hold of her head and shook it, and her brain was bouncing around in there like a BB in a box. Meg would not consider that both Tom and Bitti had drowned. After all, Tom was an excellent swimmer. In his older years, and in his youth, he was the best swimmer and fastest runner. He excelled at everything he did. And the little dog, she was an incredible swimmer too. Meg grieved at the thought of them struggling—so much so that she had to shield her eyes from the sea that held her hostage. It kept her from helping them. Her tears spilled and when she opened the faucet, there was no stopping it.

Meg had been wandering out there alone for three days. A little boat in a massive sea. Reaching overhead, Meg called out Tom's name until her brittle voice gave way, and she became silent. Meg grasped the matter of fact. It had been three days since she saw Tom, miles of water separated them, and this could be where their story ended.

She held her right fist to her heart. "Mea culpa, mea culpa, mea culpa," she repeated. "Three days, three days, three days. My fault, my fault, my fault."

CHAPTER FOUR

Discovery

M*oet* was the name painted on the upper deck of the 150-foot Hargrave motor yacht. They traveled day and night. They'd left the marina in Los Sueños, Costa Rica, in May and stopped briefly in Panama City. From Panama, *Moet* had cruised the Yucatán Sea, spent a week in Isla Mujeres, where friends flew in for a visit. *Moet* continued on, traveling the waters off Cuba. They were in no hurry. In June, the Yucatán Sea and the waters off the coast of Cuba were usually calm. Their final destination was the West Indies. The first mate, Antonio, squatted on the deck of the yacht, taking yet another smoke break while he thought of his sweetheart, whom he hadn't seen since they left Panama. Captain German Veneto was at the helm when something caught his eye off the starboard side of the vessel. A body draped lifelessly on a floating teak chair.

At first, the yacht's owner, Mariana Wells, didn't believe him. Her captain had made mistakes. He didn't see things or pay attention to detail. He misjudged at docking and fuel consumption, which had nearly gotten them in trouble two times. But it was true. A man and a little dog were nearly immersed in their path. Aboard *Moet*, they found it shocking that they hadn't run over the two of them. As the yacht approached the bodies, a running light picked up on the reflectors on their life jackets. That's how he caught a glimpse of them in the moonlight. The first mate confirmed a severely injured man and the cutest nearly drowned pup clinging to his neck in a hot-pink life vest. German moved the throttles to neutral.

Cupping his hands to his mouth, Antonio called out to the man from the swim platform. When he got no reply, he buckled his preserver and slipped into the black water. The current was minimal, and snagging the man around the neck of his life vest with the hook was an easy task. Once he had control of the man and the dog, he guided their bodies to the boat, and then the two of them, Antonio and German, pulled them aboard and onto the swim platform. Mariana watched the rescue from overhead. The rescued man's breathing was shallow. Antonio laid him out on his back, put his mouth over the rescued man's, and began. As he had been taught, Antonio counted between his breaths. He had only done this once before, for an old man on the street. This patient was overwhelmed by exposure. The sea wrinkled his skin. His lips and face were dreadfully sunburned, so much so that it may have permanently scarred him. If he weren't in such great physical shape, he might not have survived his ordeal. When his breathing became more profound, Mariana brought towels to dry him and put small amounts of fresh water on his lips.

The dog lay panting, but she took the water and ice chips when Mariana offered them. The dog was white and as soft as a piece of cotton when Mariana stroked her. She had big dark eyes and a little pointed nose, and she trembled when German put the engines in gear. They checked the man's pockets for an ID and found nothing. Mariana noticed the collar on the dog with the blue microchip tag. As she carried that fur baby inside, she slipped the collar off and threw it, aiming over the rail. But she missed her shot. It fell on deck hidden in an inflatable life raft.

The first mate's exercise was weight lifting. On the top deck, he could be seen and heard at sunrise bench-pressing weights in *Moet*'s well-equipped open-air gym. When Antonio lifted the weights over his head, he repeated words that caused him to stutter. He would say them over and over until he succeeded. But then he would fail again when he had to say the same words to German, his boss. Antonio studied nutrition. He ate multiple times a day on a diet of animal protein and low-carbohydrate grains. While his goliath physique was intimidating, Antonio had a sweetness and goodness about him. He was a gentle man who had been taught honesty and loyalty by example from his father. As a young boy, Antonio had been shy, stuttering when speaking and lacking the confidence it took to look a man in the eye. His mother's pushing and scolding only made things worse for young Antonio.

As a teen, he'd found a job in a boatyard in Panama City, sweeping floors after school. The owner took a liking to him and put him to work to earn enough money to buy smokes. After five years, he became proficient at diagnosing and rebuilding engines, and when Antonio's father passed, Antonio got hired on *Moet*. His one and only real job, *Moet* became his home. Although Mariana knew his minor flaws, she recognized his caring nature and qualities. She was pleased to have Antonio part of *Moet*'s small crew.

Antonio carefully rinsed the rescued man's body with the freshwater hose to remove the salt. He effortlessly slung the man over his shoulder and carried him to the crew's cabins at the stern of the boat. Antonio unlocked a vacant one that had once belonged to the chef and laid him on the rug on the floor. He removed his wet clothing, dried him, and moved him up on the bed. Antonio believed that crew members needed to watch out for one another, like family. Many times there was no one else. It was a lonely life, but with a job on a yacht like *Moet*, where they treated a person well and the pay was good, things could be ok.

Mariana returned with aloe for the man's skin, and after she blotted him dry, she applied it with a gentle circular motion with the tips of her fingers on the sunburned, raw areas. Mariana also brought a carafe with ice water and an insulated mug of chicken soup and set these by his bed. They covered the man's naked body with a freshly laundered sheet and put a light blanket at the foot of the bed. She noted that he wore no briefs. Meg had told Tom that one day he would have an accident and be found without them. But no underwear was the least of Tom Trumbo's problems that day. Antonio and Mariana had done all they could for him, so they left him to sleep.

Although her daughter objected, Mariana traveled alone on the yacht. Friends and family visited for a few weeks, coming aboard last port, flying out the next. They played with all the toys in the water that the motor yacht *Moet* had to offer. Being the first mate that he was, Antonio made sure all of her guests had an unforgettable visit. They screamed their lungs out while he pulled them around *Moet* on a banana they stored below in the boat garage. After they ate her food and drank her wine, there were no words from them until next time. When they left, Mariana received no family news, no birthday or holiday greeting cards from any of them. She was a very wealthy, lonely woman, and discovering the man and the dog gave her hope that life could get better for her.

German's course took them from Central America to the south of Cuba and then to the north coast of the Dominican Republic for a stop at a resort that Trump had built. From there, they would cross the deepest parts near the Caribbean Trench to Puerto Rico, the Virgin Islands, and through the West Indies to Tobago. While Tobago lay in the longitude and latitude of the hurricane belt, most of the storms originated off Africa and turned northwest. The storms rarely affected Tobago and the nearby island of Trinidad. It was *Moet*'s journey's end to spend the hurricane season there. While the boat was docked there, Mariana could fly home to Portugal while the crew would take turns staying with *Moet* or taking a holiday.

The next day Mariana rose early. She made herself a breakfast of smoked salmon with a warm toasted bagel and cream cheese and capers. She added a slice of ripe tomato, and the bagel crunched when she bit into it, and the capers fell out on the floor. Her small staff's abilities left much to be desired in the galley since her chef had left, so she did her own cooking. She wrote on her list of things to do in the Dominican Republic to hire a chef and get someone to clean. She'd had a talented chef, Camilla. Even though her imagination for culinary delights was limitless, she was young and slender and pretty, and that was the problem. Just one of them.

Mariana had lost her husband to Camilla, that pretty chef Mariana wanted to forget. Mariana searched for the love and companionship that she missed in her life. She was seeking not just sex but a good man and a friend. A role her husband had never played. He was just the father of her only child. The last night could be her answer to the loneliness.

Having breakfast where she could watch the action in the water and the birds darting in and out around *Moet* made Mariana's mornings. She tossed pieces of the leftover bagels into the air, and birds played the game and swooped in to grab them. German and Antonio stood by, each with a stink eye. Along with the birds came their droppings, which stained the paint on the boat.

Mariana's thoughts strayed to the dog. How old was the little bitty thing that slept in her cabin? She speculated about the rescued man's story. Is he a fugitive? She answered her own question. Hardly, having arrived with a dog wrapped around his neck. But what if he *is* a fugitive? The thoughts of being carried off to her cabin in the grip of a younger bad boy piqued Mariana's interest and brought a devious smile to her face.

Mariana conjured up the idea that fate had brought the two of them to her boat. There was no news of crafts lost at sea. But then her captain, German, didn't pay much attention to those things on his radio. His main concern was marine weather. She admitted to herself that she hadn't pushed German to search for news.

German joined her up top. He came with the news that the man was awake.

"His skin—it is, like, charred. Like the crisscross on a steak on a barbecue," he said. He wrinkled up his mouth and nose. "It will peel and heal, but he may have scars. I wonder how long he was out there bobbing around."

Tom's skin was naturally very dark, but his exposure to the burning sun, repeating whitecaps, and salty sea had levied a high tax on his body. When the wave came up, there had been no time for an additional application of sunblock. And luckily for the pink-skinned dog, she had been shielded from the sun beneath Tom's preserver.

Although German proudly took the credit with Mariana, Antonio was the kind soul that had made up a concoction of water, maple syrup, and salt in a jug for the man to drink to replenish his electrolytes. The maple syrup fulfilled his body's demand for sugar and potassium.

"Antonio made him breakfast with coffee, but he didn't eat much," German announced. "He doesn't speak Spanish." German threw his arms in the air with frustration.

"He keeps saying, 'No Spanish. English.' I asked him where he came from. Did he fall off a boat or what? Were there others? We asked him his name, and he stands there like a dummy."

Tom didn't understand, or he just didn't know.

Mariana's phone rang. She answered and walked out and away from German and into the salon. Thanks to *Moet*'s sixty-inch dual-antenna satellite domes, she had connections wherever she traveled. She had TV, phone, and internet anywhere in the world with the proper converters. Motor yacht *Moet* had them all. Her girlfriend Hulia called to confirm that she had purchased her airline tickets and was flying into the Dominican Republic for a visit that week to meet up with *Moet* at a marina near Punta Cana.

"Oh no." Mariana slumped forward with tightened fists; with all the lifesaving going on, Hulia's visit had slipped her mind. It could interfere with her plans. She ended the call, biting her lip as she paced the deck, wondering how she could put Hulia off. Mariana found herself always scheming.

Her Rolex said time to check on the patient. First, Mariana went to her suite to see the pup that had stolen her heart. Last night when she placed her on the king-sized bed, the dog had kept her distance far on the other side from Mariana. During the night, the puppy had passed out, whimpering and moving her paws in the bed. Mariana assumed she was reliving her harrowing experience in the water, a dog who couldn't tell her story. She had secrets and worried about her people. Did she have any idea that Tom lay injured a hundred feet away at the stern of the boat? If the dog didn't know, Mariana decided to keep it a secret for now.

The dog still hadn't eaten the raw chicken Mariana put out for her last night. Last night it had smelled like a fresh glass of milk, but now a sour smell filled the room. The dog spread out comfortably with her back legs sprawled out like a frog. She also curled up and spent a lot of time with her nose in her butt. Mariana had never owned an animal before. She presumed that's what dogs did. When Mariana moved toward her, the dog became alert and expressed concern. She expected someone else. If Meg had been there, Meg would have greeted her with a high-pitched voice and scratched her body vigorously. It would have caused her to roll on the bed and then smile—one lip up, then the other. Her master was Meg, and until now, they had never been apart.

Mariana named her Chandon. It would go with the yacht and the tender. It was motor yacht *Moet*, its tender, *Bubbles*, and now Chandon, its dog.

"It is all perfect." Except for the chicken, so she tossed it overboard.

Mariana smiled, for in Mariana's mind, everything should be perfect.

She stood before her mirror and primped her makeup and hair. Puckering her full, pouty lips, she added a coat of creamy red lipstick. Mariana opened her eyes wide. She wished they were blue, like Camilla's. She brushed black mascara on her lashes, which were still thick and naturally curled. Like Tom, she had been born with dark skin. She rubbed in two dots of a tinted sunscreen. She usually wore her wavy, brown hair cascading over her shoulders and down her back as she did that day. Other times she gathered it up on the top of her head to reveal high cheekbones and the smoothness of her skin. The owner of *Moet* was an exotically elegant woman.

Tom's cabin was smaller than Mariana remembered, but she rarely went there. The cabins were comfortable, but they needed redecorating. Each had a single bed, a small desk that also served as a table, and a private head and shower. There were no portholes or lamps. There was not enough room for a big man, like Antonio, but the cabin was adequate for Tom. It had belonged to Camilla, her chef. Mariana knocked at the door. He didn't answer, and then after a few moments, she tapped again. Still, no answer, so she called out to him, and then she boldly cracked the door. He was sleeping again.

Should I be in here? She turned to leave, and then she hesitated. It is my boat, after all, and we did save his life. I am here to see if he's ok, she convinced herself.

She had saved his life, and so far, she hadn't considered the ramifications of that. Let a soul do you a favor and they will be your lifelong friend. The route of her thinking came from David Carradine's television show, *Kung Fu*. Once you save a life, you own it. You are responsible for them forever. Was this the beginning and all Mariana needed to justify what might come next for the two of them?

Mariana judged him maybe fifty or fifty-two. In good shape, good enough that he had survived the ordeal that brought him to her. His well-formed biceps and chest were not like Antonio's but had just enough definition to be clutched by her loving hands.

She guessed correctly that he was an American of Italian descent, dark olive skin and dark-brown, thick hair that lay in curls around his forehead and ears. His covers were drawn below his waistline. He didn't have much hair on his chest, but the beginnings of the pubic hair that grew lower on his body attracted her. A warm flush swept over her and onto her shoulders. She had been with men but never sensed an instantaneous bond. Lost in the moment and not letting her eyes wander further, she wondered about the color of his eyes. Then he opened them. Oh my Lord. His eyes were open and staring up at her. She drew back and blushed at the sight of them. Their moment lasted for what seemed like a long time. Just long enough to see that his eyes were not brown but the color of waters she had seen in the Caribbean and were piercing like eyes of Jeffrey Hunter in the 1961 production of *King of Kings*.

When Tom stared up at her with that red-brown complexion and those blue eyes, Mariana became spellbound. He returned her intrusion, wondering, who? What? And where? He continued to wake up and came into the moment, opening his eyes, startled to find her there. Mariana started to speak slowly, adding English to her Spanish dialect. She spoke more English than she let on. It was her safeguard. How was he feeling? Was he comfortable? Was he in need of anything? His worried eyes asked her, Where am I? A yacht—he could see that—but where? Being a modest man, when Tom realized he was mostly naked, he grabbed at his sheet. It was their first meeting, and Mariana approved.

Mariana brought in *Moet*'s uniform polos and pants, extras of Antonio's, and hung them in the closet. Then she left him to himself. On her way up to the salon, she smiled and winked at her reflection in the mirror in the companionway stairs. But in passing she thought she saw her heart on her arm and said to herself, "Stop that."

Tom slept in his cabin for two more days. On the day Tom was ready to meet the world, he showered and shaved and dressed in the crew's uniform. Tom examined the large patches of raw skin on his cheeks and the tops of his shoulders. The purple scratches on his neck said a bird had attacked him in flight.

Tom came on deck, pulling up on the ladder, his muscles still aching. German was up in the bridge, and Tom climbed one more flight to be with him.

"I met your boss," Tom said with a nod.

German knew the word *boss* when he said it and responded, "*Sí*, Boss Lady," and barely smiled. That would be the one and only time that German smiled at Tom.

At the same time, the boss lady called on the phone for German to come to talk with her. German nudged Tom and took his two fingers and pointed them into Tom's eyes then out to sea. Tom got it; he had to watch. German left the bridge. Within a few minutes, another crew member unknown to Tom appeared.

The crew member, a young man in his midthirties, pointed at his own chest.

"I, ca, ca, ca, ca ca ca capitán ahora." He was taking over. Tom's eyes were no longer needed. Tom immediately felt sorry for the man, since he had an apparent speech impediment. He struggled with a word he had to use so often. Tom wanted to touch his shoulder and tell him to slow down.

He stood tall, much taller than Tom, and when Tom was next to him, the man could see clear over the helm with a full view of the bow. Tom compared his own hands to the crew member's hands, which were as large as a baseball glove. The rest of his body had evidence of serious weight training too. It was this crew member's shirt Tom was wearing.

"*Cómo te llamas?*" the crew member asked.

Tom understood the question; he knew that much Spanish. Tom raised his shoulders in bewilderment as German had reported.

"This is nuts." His thumb pointed to his chest as he pulled a name out of a hat and said,

"*To-mas, To-mas*, I'm *To-mas*." Then he smiled confidently.

That sounded like a decent Spanish name. Sturdy and modern. So Tom became *To-mas*. That's all he knew, but it was a beginning. Whether he knew his real name or not, no one could tell. Antonio excitedly reported to the boss lady and German that the mystery had been solved. Their new mate's name was *To-mas*, and until they could figure out what to do about him, they needed to find him something to do. A man needed a job to keep him out of trouble.

Antonio volunteered to show him the ropes in Yacht Cleaning 101. The first job he gave him was to replace every last one of the burned-out decorative lights that hung from the tip of the bow of the vessel to the stern. A 180-foot undesirable task that Antonio picked to hand off to Tom. There was always a spot on *Moet* that had to be cleaned and polished. Day after day, they labored from dawn to dusk till the work was done. Tom learned fast, and they guessed it came naturally. It all came easy to him, like he had done it before—and of course, he had. Tom got the going rate that included meals and computer time.

Tom had toured yachts before at boat shows. He had walked through them in awe. Mirrored-ceiling cabins with connecting heads. They had galleys with granite countertops and full-sized refrigerators. Each had more luxurious living rooms and dining rooms with crystal chandeliers hanging above them, where families of twelve could sit for dinner. The engine rooms were factories with diesel engines producing power and large fuel tanks providing the fuel to travel long distances without stopping. Their multiple generators supplied electricity to the entire yacht.

A yacht the size of *Moet* required a larger crew than what it had. That surprised Tom. Even though Tom Trumbo didn't know his own name, he knew enough to see that there were opportunities for him on this incredible vessel. Tom loved the sea life. His friends would die for a gig like this. His friends, if he had any, must be wondering what had happened to him.

"People don't just show up on a yacht, get a job, and motor away." But that was exactly what Tom Trumbo did.

CHAPTER FIVE

Best Laid Plans

Meg shouldn't have been following the boat in the distance. It was gone. Meg did not know how to plot a course, but she had the sun for direction during the day and her compass at the helm. With one GPS operating, she could set the autopilot and keep a straight short-term course. There were charts onboard for Mexico and the Caribbean. Meg got them and spread them out flat in the flybridge. After she estimated her position, a compass heading north-northeast should take her home to the Keys.

Meg knew it to be mandatory to stay twelve miles off Cuba's shore. The mountains she saw from *Tori's Seacret*'s starboard side told her she had broken the law. Her question was how far had the boat drifted after the wave? Crossing the Gulf Stream could mean a northeasterly shift and affect where she came ashore, but by then, Meg would have cell service and be in the vicinity of other boats.

The flare gun was in the drawer under the helm. If she encountered a boat along the way, she could use it. Her empty belly growled, so she woofed down a couple cans of chicken, but her throat was so dry she almost choked on it as it stalled at the base of her esophagus. It frightened her into drinking more water. She showered on the back of the boat and dressed in clean shorts and a T-shirt.

Meg met challenges head-on. She never quit. At dusk, Meg set herself up with water and coffee and favorite music from Tom's iPad. She listened to country music by Ronnie Millsap, and Ronnie cried out into the night.

She thought she was the only one listening. They were whiney, sad songs about broken hearts. Turning up the volume drowned out the swishing of waves hitting the bow. Hearing the words wasn't crucial, because she knew all of them and the melody by heart. It didn't take long to become depressed. There were no tears left. Her body wanted to have a drink. Her brain said that might lead to more. Her body said again, please, let's have a drink. The brain won when it said, that may end up badly, Meg.

Meg had read the instructions on the flare gun twice. After all their discussions about traveling armed, now she wished they had brought a real weapon. The chances of having to declare and surrender your firearm in some countries bothered him. When Meg had been preparing for Mexico, the recommendation was don't bring one. Fines could be hefty and confiscation of your vessel a possibility and an awful thought. Tom had chosen to leave the weapons at home. Right or wrong, Tom figured that a straight shot from the flare gun into an intruder's chest would be deterrent enough.

The hours dragged by, this time no sleeping or dreaming. Perspiration collected on her forehead. Thankfully, the boat's movement added a breeze. When Meg thought of Tom and Bitti, her greatest fear stepped forward that she might spend the rest of her days searching. Like a mother whose child was taken from her, Meg's heart would forever be empty. The songs were over. Quiet was around Meg, except for the seabirds. Gulls gliding silently alongside her, a random chirp in the air. An albatross followed low, hanging back not far behind. In the moonlight, three massive prehistoric forms circled like vultures high above her. They were frigate birds. These seabirds traveled great distances far from land in search of food. Meg hoped she wasn't the night's prey.

Meg's eyelids were heavy. She had to drive and watch and then rest whenever she could. The silence added spookiness to the ride, and thoughts of catastrophes filled her mind. She remembered an eighty-foot sailboat that hit a whale and sank. All were lost on a cargo ship off Jacksonville, and the massive containers were left floating around at sea. Then the sad movie about a sailboat caught up in a storm where only one survived. They were all documented occurrences. Meg had never dwelled on these things until a tragedy happened to her, and now it was her turn. In these moments

Meg became self-centered. No longer thinking of Tom and Bitti, only of herself. She would punish herself later for that. Her situation gave cause for a Mayday call if she had a radio that worked. Mayday calls signaled life-threatening circumstances. She'd learned that calling in a Mayday to the coast guard if none existed caused a problem. You'd get a stern talking-to by the captain of the coast guard cutter and maybe a fine. But, Meg thought, at least you'd be safe.

Meg rarely drove the boat; when she did, Tom corrected her a lot. That frustrated him, and it bugged Meg, so she didn't drive much. But now there were no corrections or complaints, and she could make all the mistakes she liked and learn from them, just like he had.

Based on when they'd left Key West and adding the days she had been alone, the calendar said June 30. The moon's shape was near full. This June night, the sea had large, smooth-rolling waves not short, choppy ones. Time could be measured between them. *Tori's Seacret* moved along slowly, up and over and down, up and over and down, up and over and down each wave. The glimmer of the moonlight caused the spray off the bow to sparkle like crystals on a chandelier. It occurred at regular intervals, and she could count on them. Through the sparkles, Meg saw the second boat. Yes, and it was large. Not too large, a yacht all lit up with twinkling lights draped from the tip of the bow to the stern. It was too small to be a cruise ship. No mistaking it as it moved east over her wake.

Meg slipped off the captain's chair and up to the tuna tower. *Tori's Seacret* rocked back and forth like a slow ring of a church bell. She inserted a flare into the barrel, closed it, and pulled back the hammer until it clicked. It was cocked and ready to fire. She raised the gun over her head, pointed it straight up into the night's sky, and pulled the trigger. Whoosh! The burning flame skyrocketed high above her until it was too high to see. She had a brief good feeling and took a deep breath when her heart let her. Something positive had happened. She loaded three additional flares and fired them. Tom had told her how to fire the gun, and she surprised herself that she did it without a hitch. Meg said to herself, I can do this. I will survive.

When Meg saw the heights that it reached, anyone within three miles could see it. Meg picked up the radio and called to the yacht.

"This is sport fisher *Tori's Seacret* calling the motor yacht off my stern, heading east. I repeat, this is sport fisher *Tori's Seacret*. Do you copy?" The radio screamed a horrible scratchy message at her. She grabbed at the squelch dial. No result. The radio had no more to say to her.

Meg repeated her message several times, switching to alternate channels. No one was listening, or if they were, her radio couldn't receive. From her perch, Meg could see the yacht continuing to move away and east of her. The next question: Was it wise to take a chance and try and catch it with no electronic aids? Not being able to read the water in the dark, she could find shallows and run aground. Meg watched the lights for as long as she could see them and fired flares five more times. The little twinkling lights got smaller and smaller and then disappeared. She wondered if they were having a party. Her eyes filled up to the brim, and then the tears puddled up and down and into her mouth and over her jaw. She thought she should have gone after them.

When Meg climbed from the tower to the helm, her leg slipped through the rung on the ladder, and she grimaced as she fell hard on her groin. It hurt bad, but she also felt relief that she hadn't fallen all the way into the cockpit on her head. Meg got herself off the ladder and into the flybridge and wrapped herself in a beach towel. The compass confirmed her heading. She shivered, but her body became accustomed to the humid air. *Tori's Seacret* continued at slow speed on autopilot. The Lord took the helm when Meg fell asleep.

Her eyes opened to an interruption in the rhythm of *Tori's Seacret*'s smooth path. A bump on the boat? Another bump, then a jolt, then moving again. The next sound. A man's gruff voice. She peeked and saw a small, single-engine, open fishing boat about twenty-five feet long tied at her stern. There were two of them speaking. Hairs stood up on her neck. As they boarded, Meg opened the door to the area under the helm, climbed in, and waited.

Her lungs found it small and stuffy under there. She held the flare gun close to her and knew what had to be next for her intruders, and she put the last flare she had in her pocket in the barrel. Her pulse pounded in her head, and she called on the Lord a second time. When Meg shot off the gun, trying to signal the yacht, she'd never considered she might be asking for trouble. Not knowing how many more there were, she couldn't know one flare would be enough. And could she shoot an unsuspecting soul because he'd answered her distress call?

Ten years ago, when she and Tom made their West Indies trip, a story surfaced about a distress call from a pleasure boat off the coast of Haiti. Help came, they took what they wanted, killed the boat's passengers and crew, and set the boat on fire.

Knowing she had company aboard, Meg pushed the door forward and crept out of the helm compartment. Meg couldn't see anyone in the cockpit. She positioned herself forward of the helm and knelt on the deck, where she had a clear view of the top of the ladder. No one coming up could see her. Meg held the flare gun poised to fire. A voice called up; it got louder as he came closer.

"Hello, hello. Is there anyone up here?" The words were Spanish. A decision needed to be made. Respond or shoot now.

A man in a beret climbed up first, an older man with a beard, and following behind him was a young boy. Meg lost her chance, and that put them fast upon her. Tom might have fired, but for Meg, firing a flare gun into the face of an old man was not something she could do.

The old man's hands said, I surrender. When he saw she had the gun pointed at him, he may have done anything to keep her from blowing all three of them up including the boat. Once Meg turned over the flare gun, they didn't speak, and he led her down to the cockpit. The big-eyed boy followed behind.

The man pulled a chart from his top pocket, unfolded it, and pointed. Meg got it instantly. She and *Tori's Seacret* were going to Cuba. Meg had no options. She could only hope that where they were taking her was better than where she had been. The boy climbed into the mate's chair. The old man offered her the helm, but Meg shook her head no and moved aside. With his boat tied at *Tori's Seacret*'s stern, the man pushed the throttles forward. He didn't need the chart or even the compass. He had done this before. A rescue by someone who knew the way in the dark agreed with her. The smell of rain was all around them. It felt refreshingly cool. His eyes found hers, and he gave Meg a nod and a quick thumbs-up. Meg rendered a hopeful smile and nodded back at him.

CHAPTER SIX

Moet and Her Crew

Mariana had to convince German that they could use another crew member on board. While Tom had no recollection of his past, eventually, he would come to find news on the internet about a man missing at sea. He would add it all up, and he would have questions. They should have called the US Coast Guard. But she didn't push it, and German didn't care. He had his agenda, and getting involved with delays with the coast guard was not part of it.

"We could decide to pay him and put him ashore when we get to Luperón or near Puerto Plata. Then we would be done with him," German said as he leaned his protruding round belly against the galley counter. "We got him out of a jam," he added while carving a piece of his lunch out of his mouth with an old toothpick he kept behind his ear.

Mariana didn't comment. German's lack of fair play disgusted her. She, too, had an agenda, and that was for Tom to stay. So Mariana changed the subject, and they both got what they wanted. She told German to get Tomas a cell phone and a passport. He needed to have papers. Fake documents could be had easily from the right people, and German knew them. He didn't refer to them as *fake* documents. He called them a word in Spanish that meant *supplemental*. When big yachts like *Moet* came to port, they could get about anything they wanted through the dockmaster's office. The best of the best liquor, fine wines, meats, caviar, and Cuban cigars were available to them. Women and drugs were also accessible. German obeyed and

39

emailed his source in Punta Cana to have Tomas's *supplemental* documents waiting when they arrived at the marina.

German had been *Moet*'s captain for nearly three years. The original captain he replaced had suddenly resigned after an incident that occurred while they were in Costa Rica. *Moet* spent a lot of time there. Costa Rica's countryside stretched vast and rich with vegetation. The coastal areas were lower in elevation; the inland regions were rugged and mountainous and filled with dormant volcanos. The beaches were varied from the whitest white sand to the blackest black. Tourists were welcomed with discounts and complimentary tours by the department of tourism. Local people did their part and cooked their regional recipes for tourists on the streets outside their homes. A beautiful country and a safe place to visit.

Many of the wealthy invested money in Costa Rica. They bought homes and lived there, seasonally. Sportfishing boat owners shipped their boats on large barges to Costa Rica and flew in to enjoy the fishing in the fertile Pacific Ocean. San Jose was the capital and its largest city. It boasted fine dining, shopping, and cultural events. One of the favorite destinations of Mariana and her husband, Max Wells. Each year they visited Costa Rica while cruising on *Moet*. One of the best things for boaters was the fact that Costa Rica lay beneath the hurricane belt and was never threatened by them.

While they were there, Mariana checked in to the Costa Rica Clinica for Women, a well-known clinic that wealthy South and North American women went for lifts, breast implants, and other rejuvenation procedures. The clinic offered a cleansing of the body and mind. Alcoholic beverages and smoking were not allowed, and a dietician planned their meals.

While recuperating at the clinic, the clientele played bridge and chess and read books. The clinic invited vendors to visit from Europe to set up trunk shows featuring designer dresses from France, shoes and handbags from Italy, and Tiffany from New York. As much as Max loved his fishing and time with the guys, Mariana loved shopping. And the trunk shows gave her first choice to see and wear new styles and accessories from over the pond. When the ladies were healed and ready to be seen in public, the clinic would send them in a limo to downtown San Jose for a degustation meal and their first glass of wine. The ladies returned home with their new skin and eyes, five pounds thinner. The first time Mariana visited the clinic, it was her birthday, and she was fifty-two years old, and when the doctor examined her, he said to her seriously, "It is time. Yes, you are ready."

Max wanted Mariana to get implants, although she didn't agree. But she went along, and on the day of her appointment, she carried twenty thousand dollars cash in a legal-sized yellow envelope under her arm. It was the lifestyle they lived.

Moet docked at the marina in Los Sueños on the Pacific during that time. Max and his friends came for fishing and hunting. While the men played, Mariana entertained their wives, flaunting her wardrobe and jewelry, making them green.

German worked on *Moet* as a crew member. He chartered fishing boats to take the men to the ripest fishing spots. They would fish in the deep, trolling over mountains on the ocean floor. Game fish swam up to feed on the baitfish that gathered there. German also hired seasoned guides and took them into the rainforest to hunt boa and python for sport. Each trip, the men returned carrying a big one wrapped around a post for the locals to make purses and boots from the skin. Mariana had several in her closet.

Max liked German because German could get things done for him. He could get Max anything he wanted and made Max a big shot in front of his friends. He was arrogant and didn't care. German knew people through his former employer in Medellin, Colombia. While German worked there, he saw a lot, and when German saw too much, he sought a career change. He changed his name, began traveling to other countries, and blended in away from his past. Unfortunately, that's when *Moet*'s captain hired him.

On that particular trip to Costa Rica, they hunted boa in the jungle the day before they left port. Wet backpacks and muddy boots were heaped in a pile in the storage area at the stern of the boat. Out twenty-five miles from shore, the captain checked the area at the stern of the boat. A strap from one of the backpacks got stuck hanging out in the door of a hatch. He pulled on it and released the hatch door. A total surprise and without any warning, a pit viper sprang out at him, nearly six feet. Its jaws were open 180 degrees, and its one-inch fangs sank into an artery in the captain's arm with such force the blood squirted out like a fountain across the deck. Everyone standing there scattered. The captain screamed in pain.

"Ah! Ah! Ah! Snake! I've been bitten by a snake."

A frightening experience and surprise for everyone aboard, except German. The captain's shrieks reverberated throughout the boat. He couldn't be quieted. Mariana and Max, who sat in the cockpit directly above, drew back when they saw the snake attack. Once the snake released its hold on the captain's arm, it coiled into a corner inside the hatch, waiting to strike its next victim. No one knew what to do. The captain crouched then lay incapacitated. German responded and ran to him.

"*Terciopelo!*" Now German screamed. He knew it. A fer-de-lance, a pit viper found in Central America and other rainforest areas of the world. It was common knowledge among the medical industry that 50 percent of venomous snakebite deaths in the world were due to the bite of the fer-de-lance. Once the victim was bitten, swelling and blistering occurred and then tissue death—then amputation or death. Time was critical. German acted fast. He knew to create a tourniquet on the captain's arm to confine the poison. He applied pressure to stop the life-threatening blood loss. He immediately radioed and got air transport to take the captain to the hospital in San Jose. But even with antivenom and experienced doctors, he ended up losing his arm to the elbow.

After that incident, German was promoted to captain. His first official job was to lasso the viper and get it off the boat, or Mariana wouldn't travel. The next day Captain German showed up for work with an eighteen-karat gold anchor on a thick chain around his neck. He devotedly wore his gaudy prize on his hairy chest under his captain's uniform.

German observed Mariana. He was smitten by her. He had thoughts that didn't belong in his head and dreams. He would risk his life for her. And now German had. After eight years as captain of *Moet*, German stood where he wanted to be, but neither Mariana nor Max knew his personal history, and that was probably a mistake.

CHAPTER SEVEN
Cuba

Motoring along, the young boy, who spoke excellent English, told Meg about their destination. Marina Los Morros, the smallest in all of Cuba. It was positioned south of Cape San Antonio. Key West boaters spoke of it on the charts. It sat on the west-southwest tip of Cuba on the Guanahacabibes Peninsula and could be a midway point to Mexico, although Americans were not legal there. He proudly said he'd learned in school that the land's name came from the aboriginal Guanahatabey. The old man added that his recent ancestors were born among the tribe. Meg tried to calculate the years in her head to figure if that could even be possible. The last knowledge of them being in the sixteen hundreds. The Indians were hunters and gatherers who lived in caves and ate fish. Their decline began with the invasion of the Spaniards. In the end, the Indians disappeared in Cuba due to butchery, slavery, disease, and suicide. Ultimately, the peninsula became part of a famous biosphere reserve.

They were grandfather and grandson, Jhosep and Juan. Jhosep, who spoke good enough English, told Meg about the Maria la Gorda Dive Center, located seventy kilometers from the marina. The name came—legend had it, and he confirmed it—from Maria, a rather voluminous gal kidnapped in the Caribbean by pirates and brought to their base on the peninsula. Maria had cooked, cleaned, mended their britches, and patched them up after drunken brawls. Research might tell one that there were very many renditions of her story. The pirates called her Fat Mary, and when Mary died, to honor her memory, they buried her beneath the tallest indigenous palm tree on the bay along with a pirate's treasure.

"Even though the tourists keep digging, it's never been found." He let out a raucous bray of laughter. These were the stories that he told. The boy confirmed he had heard them before. All the way, Meg's eyes were fixed on the lighthouse on the cape and the rotating beam guiding them in.

Once they tied *Tori's Seacret* securely and set the fenders on the long dock, Meg got out a splitter to plug the fifty-amp power cord into the marina's thirty-amp stanchion. She powered down the generator, and they went to the office to fill out paperwork. It was still dark as she followed behind them and tried to use her phone; there was no service. Jhosep pulled out a form from a drawer in the marina office and filled in the date for her: July 1, 2018. A memorable date for Meg—her daughter's wedding anniversary. Oh, her daughter, Carol. She must be so worried and upset. In all these days, she had never given her a thought. Meg signed the bottom of the form, Meghan Trumbo.

"That's good enough for now. Let's go rest," he said.

Immigration would be in the morning when the Cuban authorities made their way to Marina Los Morros. They only came once a week. Afterward, Meg headed to the boat, and Juan pulled her in another direction. He was a kid, wide awake, and seeking company.

"No, I'm sorry, I need to go to the boat now," Meg said, but he followed behind her on the bank. Meg gave in and sat with him awhile on a swing outside of the office, where she learned Juan lived in Havana. He was here briefly visiting his grandfather, who worked and lived at the marina. They had been out fishing that night when they saw her flares, and only because the sea set still were they able to get to her so quickly.

"My grandfather can take you and the *Tori's Seacret* to Havana, where dockage is safe. There is much to see and do. Not like here." Juan read her mind as she appraised the desolate area. Meg understood that rural areas in Cuba were devastated from hurricanes, one after another, year after year.

Meg smiled at him, and her heart wished that could be true. The prospect got her thinking. She had plenty of cash in her safe, and she wondered about the exchange rate and how long it would take to get to Havana. She had gotten off the beaten path. Not in her plan to come, of all places, to Cuba. In a big city like Havana, though, she could access the internet, get in touch with the coast guard, and call her daughter to see if they had news of Tom.

Meg picked his brain. "Juan, I can't imagine that your grandfather wants to take me all the way to Havana. But thank you."

After Meg swatted five mosquitos on her legs, she sent Juan on his way to Jhosep's hut. He wanted to talk more. Rescuing an American lady on a sixty-one-foot fishing boat like *Tori's Seacret* would be a lifetime memory maker for young Juan.

"We'll talk again. I promise. I am sure I will be here awhile."

Juan gave in, still disappointed, but being an obedient child, he continued down the path. After Meg witnessed him disappear into the hut, she went to the boat.

The electric went off on the dock. Not a surprise, as it was common in the marinas in the islands. If it were not so hot, and if she had a screen for the doorway to get air and keep the bugs out, she would have roughed it and opened up. Meg started the generator starboard, the opposite of before, as Tom had taught her. What would she be without Tom? What was Meg then? She couldn't sleep. Meg made a strong cup of coffee and sat and imagined Havana from what she had heard from her friend Betsy. She got out her cruising guide and charts and started calculating.

Based on mileage, the ride from Cape San Antonio to Havana would take about eight hours. That estimation depended on the seas and weather and would use about eight hundred gallons of fuel. They'd installed new fuel gauges before they left, so they could predict accurately. Meg could have topped off her tanks there at Los Morros, but lack of boat traffic concerned her. Taking on old fuel could cause problems with clogged fuel filters and engine performance. Her next task was to figure out how she could get Jhosep to take her. Scheming and planning were bold moves for meek Meg.

Meg slept a few hours and then got up and got dressed. Marina Los Morros wasn't much better in daylight. The July day brought brutal heat with no breeze. There were no other boats except for Jhosep's and *Tori's Seacret*. There was one long two-hundred-foot disintegrating concrete dock that provided little protection from the weather and surf. The marina facilities were minimal. Finding a toilet with a seat and paper made one lucky. The office turned off the water at night; flushing in the morning was not an option. So, things piled up. Most humanitarian vessels that came in with nurses or teachers aboard were grossly offended. *Poo poo*!

Besides the small office that sat one, it had a restaurant with six tables, four chairs each, and a bar with four barstools and no alcohol except rum. In the restaurant, she ordered another cup of coffee. The menu said the restaurant served two basic meals daily. If you brought in your bottle of wine, they didn't mind or charge a cork fee. The staff consisted of one local woman who brought her six-month-old baby to work.

Cape San Antonio was a sparsely populated area. It had an internet tower, but it remained damaged. An airstrip, but no scheduled flights.

Bird-watching was a big attraction. Bee hummingbirds flittered every-where. Meg saw them frozen in flight; their invisible wings made sucking nectar from the flowers at all levels an easy job. Like mini helicopters, their motors barely humming, they moved up and down, side to side from each bloom to the next. Meg stood a long time in awe of their agility. Wild boars were the draw for hunters seeking that challenge in the jungle beyond the coast. With the beautiful water, Cape San Antonio lured drive-in tourists for the day, but it was remote and by no means a honeymoon destination.

Meg started the water maker. Where the waters were clean, the filter rarely needed servicing. A good thing, because while they had plenty of them in the engine room, she hadn't a clue on how to change one. Meg pulled on a *Tori's Seacret* T-shirt over her head, smeared on fifteen sunscreen, and went outside. She got out her boat soap, bucket, and brush from a fish box in the cockpit and began in the flybridge, working down. It kept her busy and passed the time. Salt, dirt, and bugs were everywhere. The helm was sticky, and the gauges and electronics' screens were almost unreadable. Boat cleaning was Tom's job, and it was now hers. No local dock boys were hang-ing around to make money by scrubbing boats in the middle of nowhere.

When she finished the last part of the cockpit, a man showed up on the dock next to the boat with a folder of papers. He wore dark sunglasses that didn't hide his scowl. His complexion was a ruddy brown from living his life in the sun. He didn't wear a gun, but he wore a uniform with patches that appeared official. Meg laid her brush down and smiled, said hello, and invited him onboard into the salon and the cool. He sat at the dining table and waited.

"Something to eat?"

Something to eat? Meg thought to herself. Was she supposed to make him breakfast? Or offer a bribe? She put a small can of V8 in front of him, and he drank it, but his expression never changed. Meg retrieved her passport, boat documentation, and other pertinent information. He was waiting to see her permit to enter, and he brusquely repeated the word three times. She didn't have one. How could she? He only spoke a few words of English, and just as she was beginning to try to explain in her limited Spanish vocabulary, thankfully, Jhosep tapped on the door and invited himself in.

He bent over to fit when he came through the door. He and the officer spoke, and Jhosep waved his arms and turned his body as he pointed out to the ocean and then up in the air and opened his fingers wide over his head. Meg could only imagine Jhosep was explaining to him about how he'd found her and her predicament. Finally, the officer nodded yes, he agreed, and he wrote the permit. The officer smiled because he had completed his job. Meg wanted to offer him a tip but was afraid to insult him because she didn't know how much. Jhosep's eyebrows gave Meg a negative. Tom had always dealt with that too. She thanked Jhosep, and he went off to tie up a sailboat that had just arrived in the harbor.

Jhosep's steps thundered down the dock, hopping over crevices in his path, and Meg saw a man who carried himself with purpose. He was maybe six foot five, with a build that a seaman might have. He had no limps or shuffles about his gait. His well-trimmed beard was gray, although his wiry, thick hair was still jet black. The beret added a European style. She knew he was an unforgettable character. She had met a few in her life. He was not a lover, but he was a person she would never forget. She saw him maybe as a man who spent his life in a struggle in oppression. To know him better and hear more about his life would have been compensation for her strife. But Meg had no time for that. So far, he hadn't been a man of many words, but the things he said came to be true. That was why Meg trusted him.

In the last two days, Meg had found herself doing jobs she'd never done before. Not great things but things that had been done by Tom. In the past, he'd made all the decisions, planned all the trips, and plotted the courses. He determined the time frame and the calculated fuel usage and range. Meg primarily went along for the ride. Like their lives.

Refocusing, Meg turned her attention to the new sailboat that had just come in. Its red maple leaf flag draped from its mast. It skated in smoothly on the twenty-eight-horse Volvo Penta's power. Meg planned to go to see the new sailboat crew, but the two of them came straight away to talk.

"Hello," Meg called out to them as she pulled her hair away from her eyes. "Where did you come in from?" The morning's low tide put *Tori's Seacret* six feet below the dock. Meg bent her head up to see them as they answered her.

"Havana, what a place! More than we ever expected and less. It has a fantastic skyline as you approach, but you get a surprise. Before that, we were in West Palm Beach waiting for a part."

"I am Meg Trumbo. I am here waiting for my husband."

Well, partially true. Meg didn't know why she'd said that, but to talk of the truth of the matter couldn't happen yet. Meg asked questions about any news of a missing boat. But they had nothing to offer. They went on their way up to the office to fill out paperwork and get their permit stamped. Meg saw them on their boat, hauling water and cleaning up; she went over and invited them to come to her boat for dinner. She wasn't surprised that they anxiously accepted. Meg was glad they did. They loved sailing, but they liked the conveniences of a powerboat as well, things not available on a forty-three-foot sailboat. One might consider it odd to invite strangers to your house for dinner, but it was not unusual at all in the boating life.

John and Sharon were the couple on the sailboat. High school science teachers who cruised during their summer vacations. John was squatty and thin and wore small, round glasses with an elastic band to hold them firmly on his head. His sandy-colored hair curled up at the nape of his neck with gray at his temples. They both wore long-sleeved shirts and long, lightweight pants to protect them from the sun. Sharon measured taller than John by six inches. A slender woman with shoulder-length, mousy brown hair and classic facial features, she appeared to Meg to be at least ten years younger than John. They dressed so much alike that, except for their height, they could have been twins. Meg judged them to be excellent boating buddies.

Sharon was anxious to talk. John said very little and nodded his head in agreement like a bobblehead. Sharon talked about the soccer balls and shoes and the snorkel gear they brought to the children in Havana.

"The children and people there really have nothing." She shook her head. "They were all so pleasant and thankful."

Sharon also talked about the old cars that people had managed to maintain since the fifties. John perked up when she said it. "They fixed the cars' engines and repaired and painted damaged parts. They are so resourceful."

"Do you know what these cars would be worth in the US? You see the mint ones selling at the auto auctions for a hundred thousand dollars, sometimes more. I told Sharon, Havana's like a slice out of time."

"We hired a tour guide for two hundred bucks a day."

"That US dollar?" Meg asked.

"Best money we ever spent," John added.

"Yes," Sharon responded. "We got the name of the guide through a Canadian travel agent. Others told us that you're not supposed to deal in US dollars, but our guide encouraged it. The man was outstanding and spoke English well enough for us to follow. He explained to us that many teachers in Cuba, like him, had abandoned their teaching jobs to become tour guides. They could make a lot more money. He chauffeured us in a red fifty-five Chevy, small block V-8, and stayed with us at night as late as we wanted and dropped us at the boat."

Meg knew the model but didn't understand small block V-8. If Tom were there, he would. It always came back to Tom.

"Did you get to see the show at the Tropicana?" Meg asked.

"Yes, incredible as you'd imagine, with all the colorful costumes and the music. They put a bottle of rum and shot glasses at your table. We had a great time."

Sharon continued to say that the guide had taken them to places that most tourists didn't know to go. The next day they planned on continuing around the island to Playa Ancon, about three hundred miles. At least a day and night sailing for them. The marina at Playa Ancon sat seven miles from the inland city of Trinidad. One of the must-see places in Cuba. They also talked about leaving their boat someplace safe, flying home for the school year, and then continuing their trip next year, but they all agreed that Cuba wasn't the place to do that.

Meg suggested they come to dinner at six.

At five o'clock, Meg opened a drawer in the galley and got out the only apron she had in the boat. She'd bought the apron from Vern's Grocery in Hope Town, Bahamas. Vern was a famous old-time small grocer that sold food and supplies to the transient boaters. Vern's wife baked Johnny bread it at dawn and laid it out at the checkout counter. Cruisers pushed through the doors in the morning to get theirs before it was gone. Meg tied the apron around her waist and smoothed out its wrinkles from being stuffed in a drawer since the last trip. It was fifteen years old and stained red and yellow from tomato sauce and oil. A chronicle of the meals she and Tom had made together. Sometimes Meg wore it naked for him. She got out her recipe for the sautéed fish. Her tears smeared the blue ink on the card on the counter. Could she go through with this? Have a dinner party on their boat when the love of her life and her dear, sweet Bitti could be dead? Meg had to unthink it.

But now Meg had an obligation. She cooked the meal and wrapped it in a throwaway pan. She printed off a photo on her compact portable printer of Tom holding Bitti, and she wrote her name, email address, and cell number and shoved it into her apron pocket. Meg went to the sailboat, juggling the fish and the pasta and a bottle of wine. She bent over to knock on the hull when Sharon stuck her head up from below.

"Sharon, I am sorry, but I can't have you over tonight. I already started preparing, so I cooked it. I wrapped it tightly. I think it will stay warm until dinnertime."

Sharon looked concerned. "Is everything ok? Are you not feeling well?"

"I'm fine. I may be going to Havana with the boat in the morning. I took on too much inviting you to dinner. I hope you understand. I have a big day ahead of me."

"Meg, don't worry. Honestly, we both said it was an invite we should have turned down. We're both worn out and need to be out of here early in the morning too. But John and I will enjoy the meal and the wine. Thank you so much."

Meg never gave her the photo from her pocket. But no matter, the next morning, their sailboat was gone before the sun came up. Meg found a note, thanking her for dinner, and signed, "John and Sharon Brandt, sailing vessel *Keep Learning*."

Later, when Meg saw Jhosep sweeping the dock, she asked him for information about making the trip to Havana, although she didn't ask him to take her. She asked him about the seas and the current and the approach to the marina. She assumed he had made it before. He laid down his broom and stood wide, hands on his hips, frowning at her.

"Do you plan to go alone? It's a long way, all day even with good weather and seas. The inlet at the marina is not easy without local knowledge and impossible after sunset when you can't read the water."

"I think I need to go there, but I don't want to leave the boat here."

Meg had counted on Jhosep offering to go with her. If he didn't, she would have to leave *Tori's Seacret* behind. Tom wouldn't agree with that. She knew a better option would have been taking the boat to Key West, but the thought of heading out alone was out of the question. At least once in Havana, she would have more options.

"I will take you," Jhosep conceded as he shifted from one foot to the other. "My grandson already told me. He says we need to take you. It is time for Juan to return home anyway, and with his father's permission, we will take you and the boat there. When Juan comes and stays with me, my son, Silvio, drives here by car to pick him up, but if he agrees, we will go."

They agreed between them that with Juan's father's approval and fair weather, Jhosep and Juan would take Meg and *Tori's Seacret* to Havana.

The three of them left the following day, early while the seas were calm, for the eight-hour trip to the marina near Havana. While *Tori's Seacret* had all the electronics to set a course on autopilot, she didn't know how, and even if she did, Jhosep would have chosen to drive the Viking without them. It wasn't a challenge for him. It was what he knew. Jhosep held the wheel with both wrinkled and gnarly hands. His fingerprints and the creases in his palms were filled with the toil of his life that didn't come clean when he washed them. Meg yawned and took a snooze on the bench up with them in the flybridge. At lunchtime, she prepared sandwiches and cold drinks. Juan thought it was cool to have Coca-Cola with his lunch. It was available in Havana but not in authentic Coca-Cola pop-top cans. He saved the can as a souvenir of his vacation with his grandfather.

Silvio, Juan's father, stood at the dock later that day when *Tori's Seacret* pulled into Hemingway Marina. They snaked in and around the markers that were still standing upright. Meg tossed the stern line to Silvio, and Juan tied the bow. It was a side tie for them, and Juan had the fenders set perfectly to protect the hull from the scrapes of a rough docking. But Jhosep handled her perfectly. Tom would have been proud of the way she dealt with the lines. Silvio had a big, bright, perfect smile, and he used it when he saw his son.

Juan introduced her to his father, they shook hands, and then Silvio invited her in.

"You will come to dinner at our home tonight; my wife is preparing one of our favorite meals to celebrate Juan's return and Jhosep's visit." Meg wanted to say no, but it wouldn't be right.

"Yes, thank you, that is so kind of you," Meg said. "But I have to clean up, and I have to make phone calls."

"We will come for you at eight; I took care of your paperwork. The dockmaster got your permit approved."

The best news Meg had heard all day. They said goodbye to Meg, and as the three of them walked away, Silvio smiled again at his son and rubbed the top of Juan's head two times. Silvio loved his son. Jhosep trailed a little behind his son and grandson, and Meg thought that odd from what she had seen of him. He seemed fatigued, but he was older, and it was a long day, and she felt that way too.

Meg walked up to the dockmaster's office to inquire about a telephone. The assistant dockmaster told her she could use the private phone in the office, but calls would have to be brief, and there would be an extra charge on her bill. The first call Meg made was to Tom. It rang and rang and then went to voice mail.

"Tom Trumbo. Leave a message, and I'll call you back." Hearing his voice was heartening even if it was just a recording. She made a mental note to call it again if only to listen to him say his name.

"This is me. Call me. I am at Hemingway Marina in Cuba with the boat." She left a number.

Her next call she made to her daughter, Carol. No answer. She called again. No answer, and she left a message. The following telephone call was to the coast guard office in Key West. Officer Harrington answered, and when she told him her name and the name of her boat, he responded, and he put Meg on hold. The next voice was Commander Gonzalez of the Key West sector. He knew her name and the boat immediately.

"You are an important person, Mrs. Trumbo; a lot of people are asking for you and your husband. There have been so many people calling."

"I am at Hemingway Marina in Havana. I am alone with our boat. Has there been any word on my husband, Tom Trumbo? We hit a storm and then a massive wave. That's when we were separated. We could hear the coast guard on our radio, but when we responded, we got nothing. I sent up flares, and a man in a fishing boat came and brought me and the boat to Cape San Antonio. No cell service there. She repeated herself. Now I am at Hemingway Marina, west of Havana. I just arrived with the boat today."

Meg imagined that the commander became impatient with her rambling, but she didn't care. It just all came out all at once. For the first time, a sigh of relief went through her when she told her account to a person of authority who mattered and could help her. He took all her information and repeated basic questions. Where did she make landfall? She confirmed it and repeated that she was now in Havana, Cuba, with the boat. She filled him in and again asked about her husband, Tom Trumbo. He said no. No news of him. But he said yes, their daughter, Carol, contacted them regularly; their friend JP, a commercial pilot, had rented a plane out of the Key West airport and searched the area between Key West and Cuba and Mexico. They had sent radio messages to boats in the area, but no sightings had been reported, no debris found. No news. At least until now.

The dockmaster started glancing over at her. Her time was up. Meg gave the commander the number at the marina office, and they agreed she would contact him again.

Meg went to the boat, she showered and dried and styled her hair. She sorted through her lipsticks. She had a pale-pink and a hot-pink one. Meg put a dab of the pale pink. That's all she needed from her makeup drawer; her sunburned red complexion had toned down to a golden brown, and she glowed. From her closet, Meg pulled out a light-blue dress with white starfish trim at the neck and slipped it on over her head, making sure not to catch a smear of lipstick on the neck. Meg's white flip-flops with rhinestone-studded starfish matched the dress perfectly. When Meg stood in front of the full-length mirror, the image said, "Good enough and not too glitzy" to meet the lady of the house. Meg wanted to bring a gift. She grabbed two bottles of Pinot Noir that Tom had put aboard. He always knew the best ones to buy. Ready early, Meg sat and thought about that day's trip.

Everything had moved along that day, once they left Cape San Antonio. She was busy making sandwiches for them, watching Jhosep's handling of the boat, and seeing the north coastline of Cuba. They'd seen hundreds of frigate birds circling in the sky. There must have been good fishing in the areas they passed. There were robust currents that slowed them. But there were no big fishing boats in the water. There were only a few twenty-footers like Jhosep's when they got near the land. The rest were makeshift floats made of inner tubes that locals used to take them away from the shore to find fish.

"Where are the large fishing boats?" Meg had asked Jhosep.

"Most of the people fish from the wall at the Malecon in Havana. They cannot fish when the weather is bad, and the wind blows from the north. They can't afford to buy boats. Tourists think they are there for recreation, but they fish to survive. Most don't even own a fishing rod. They use a wheel with a line and blow up condoms for bobbers."

It sounded so desperate to Meg, and it made her feel sorry for his people. A rat tap tap on the side of the boat interrupted Meg's thoughts. It was Silvio. She grabbed her bag, switched the engines' ignitions off at the panel, and locked the door.

Silvio dressed in long pants and a polo shirt. He was more handsome to her than when she'd met him earlier. He had a noticeable form to his physique, and he had a relaxed style to his demeanor. She could see that Silvio resembled his father, but he was not as tall as Jhosep. His hair was short and black, and he combed it straight back. His nose was straight, and his clean-shaven, square jaw made his black, pencil-thin mustache stand out. Meg had to work to control her blush when she met him. His squinty eyes swept over her top to bottom and up again as other men had done to her. A feeling absent from her life for a very long time. They chatted as they walked the dock to his car past workers who stopped cold to check Meg out.

Silvio opened the door to his black sedan for Meg to get in. Not a new car, but it was clean and shiny. The driver's side was on the right. Meg noticed Silvio's hand on the steering wheel. In contrast to Jhosep, he held the wheel with one hand and leaned back in his seat with his other suntanned arm out the open window. His hands were small for a man of his size. They were smooth, and the nails were freshly manicured.

The ride to Silvio and Ann's home was short and west of Havana. The home was surrounded by a faded black metal fence with arrowheads on the tops of each picket. A large gate that stood open led to a gravel driveway. When he turned in from the main road, he increased his speed, and the car tires crunched and sprayed out stones into the air. Allamanda bushes were green and full of leaves that needed trimming, and their yellow flowers framed the gate. The Poinciana trees that appeared to be on fire cascaded on both sides of the long stretch. Beyond there were eight huge, old banyan trees, four on each side with the branches growing together at the top, creating a tunnel that led to a yellow-and-white trimmed farmhouse. In the last two banyan trees were flowering bromeliads growing randomly in the braids of the trunks. A person that lived in the home had green thumbs. The house was not large. It was old but well kept. The porch that wrapped the home had rockers out front. It had a welcoming look, a place you'd like to stay and visit.

Jhosep, Juan, and Ann, Juan's mother, were lined up like toy soldiers waiting on the top step of the porch. The front door and windows were open, and the sheer white curtains were pulled aside, and the evening breezes blew through. When Meg walked up the stairs, Ann took her hand and greeted Meg warmly. Ann was about the same size as Silvio, but thinner and younger than Meg had expected her to be. Her soft brown curls that lay just beneath her ears were held in place with a plain narrow headband. The pale-pink lipstick gave the only color to her face. Meg knew right then that she'd made the right choice for her own lips. Even though Ann had lived in Cuba for several years, you could still pick up her Midwest accent, where her "Aws" were "Ahs" and sodas were pops. Meg understood why Juan spoke such perfect English.

Silvio held the screen door as they all went inside. The scent of onions sautéing in butter spread from the kitchen through the living room, even though Meg had heard Cuba cooking could be bland. When Meg walked in, her eyes were drawn to the left to the dining room. Oil paintings of all sizes and shapes dominated the walls. Every inch of the canvases was filled with vibrant brushstrokes of red, orange, green, and purple, each an affirmation of life in Cuba from the past to the present. There were scenes of men in the fields cutting sugar cane, bongos and guitar players in the streets, generously built women dancing in yellow ruffled skirts. And one of American automobiles from the fifties lined up on the street in Havana. Plain, narrow, dark-brown wood framed each masterpiece so as not to take away from the message reaching out to the viewer.

The living room was on the right. On the cream chalk-painted coffee table were lightly salted Marcona almonds from Spain. They were Meg's favorite. She knew they were costly and hard to come by and wondered where Ann got them. Next to the almonds, the eyes of the revolutionary Che Guevara stared up at her. His book, *The Motorcycle Diaries*, Meg had read it.

Ann served sangria with mango in large red wine glasses with gold trim at the base, and Ann poured half as much in Juan's Spiderman tumbler. The sangria complimented the almonds, and Meg had a hard time not making a pig of herself. She wanted to put a bunch in her handbag for later. Meg offered to help in the kitchen but restrained herself when she saw a servant as the kitchen door swung open and Ann disappeared, donning her apron, to make her final preparation for dinner. Meg knew better, and if it were her, she would want to be left alone to make everything perfect.

Ann returned to the room and stood behind Silvio's chair with her hands on the top of his shoulders. Meg asked Ann how she came to live in Havana. Silvio began to speak over her, but he stopped and let her go on.

"I came to Havana on a teacher's visa twelve years ago. I was here for six months during the winter, and while here, I met Silvio." She smiled at Silvio and rubbed his shoulders. "I loved Havana, and he helped to make it possible for me to stay longer. Soon after that, we married, and Juan was born."

"Did you continue to teach?" Meg asked.

"I did initially, but then I had a difficult pregnancy. I flew home to Chicago toward the end to be with my mother and father, and Juan was born there."

"So then does Juan have dual citizenship?" Meg asked, and Silvio interrupted.

"Juan is a citizen of Cuba."

"If Ann were to leave, could she take Juan with her?" As soon as Meg's words came out, she wanted to reach up and grab them and pull them in. She knew she'd asked a poor question, but too late, the words were out there. Juan sent a worried look when Silvio responded to Meg, "That would never happen."

Then Ann continued. "Once Juan grew old enough, I began teaching again in primary school. When school is out, and in between baseball practices, I volunteer and teach reading in the agricultural areas to workers in the evening and to older people who have no means of travel."

"Are you gone overnight?"

"When it is necessary, and when I am, I take Juan with me. He also teaches the elderly. They love him. And he is so patient with their struggling minds. When they know we are coming, the old women make him cookies. It's a treat for Juan. He gets an opportunity to talk with the workers. He can see another type of life from his."

"Ann, is it wrong for me to ask what things are allowed to be taught here in the schools? Is there any talk of religion?"

"I can tell you this. There is no talk of religion in government schools. If there is any talk of religion, it is in the home. I will give you an example of Communist teachings." Ann slid two potted plants in front of her from the coffee table. "These two plants are brought into the classroom. One plant we let God take care of and the other plant the government takes care of. Every day the students water the government's plant; they give it sunshine and fertilizer. The other plant next to it, they leave to God. And naturally, at the end of the month, God's plant dies."

Meg didn't know what to say. She had just witnessed a stunning exposé of the Communist method of teaching young impressionable minds.

Ann continued. "Silvio's position with the government has given us a good life. But the people are controlled by the party. The people have nothing except what the party decides they should have. They give us free health care, housing, and education. But what do the people do with it if they are not free to make choices?" Meg nodded her head.

"We have vouchers for food and clothing. There is very little meat and a lot of beans and rice. Our average citizen earns thirty dollars a month, and professionals make slightly more. People are not allowed to farm on their own property. The government owns most of it, the food that is grown on the farms and even the fish that swim in the sea. Countries employ our doctors and send their salaries to Cuba. Cuba sends its doctors to work in Venezuela in exchange for oil. Cuba's exportation of its doctors for hire brings home over ten billion dollars a year. Much more than tourism."

Meg listened and said, "I have read that your literacy rate is at the top of the scale. All of this is confusing to me."

"It always returns to Marxist politics, Meg. If you play by the rules, do your military time, health care and education are available to you for free. Just don't step out of line. The people are groomed for the benefit of the state."

In the position that Silvio held with the education ministry, his wife shouldn't have spoken so negatively. Meg could tell by the expression he gave Ann. But he let her continue on. Jhosep sat quietly in a large, stuffed chair that had his name on it. His when he came for his visits. Juan sat on a small, brightly upholstered stool next to his father. Juan sat waiting for his chance to talk about his adventure, but Ann put her finger up to her mouth whenever she saw him about to begin. Meg remembered those times in America long ago. Children were seen and not heard.

During dinner, Meg talked about her plan to get to the United States and then return to search for Tom. Meg gave an account of the catastrophe. Juan was wide eyed, and his mouth hung open when Meg covered the details. He hadn't known about the dog.

"We had come through a long, horrible rainstorm. We were all wet and exhausted. I had put out lunch when Tom saw the churning wave. It was far away from us, but as it got closer, it doubled in breadth and height several times. Tom reacted and pointed the bow into it, but our engines couldn't compete. I remember the boat going over, and then I was underwater. When I came up, I saw the boat had turned upright. The engines were at idle, and it rolled with the waves, and the tuna door was swinging open. I climbed on."

Silvio had questions. He had never experienced a wave. Unlike his father, he had not spent most of his older life on the sea. Jhosep chimed in that he knew others that had seen one, but most hadn't survived. Silence sat at the dinner table and made them uncomfortable. No one wanted to be frank as to their expectations that she would find her husband at all, let alone alive. But Meg had confidence that she could have hope. She told them that, on the following day, she planned to find an internet café and get her cell phone working and make more calls. Neither Silvio nor Ann could understand how this little woman had ended up here at their dining table, but it wasn't uncommon for Juan to bring home strays.

"Today, I was able to use the phone in the marina office to contact my daughter. Then I spoke with the commander at the Key West coast guard station. I have to get in touch with him tomorrow. I am hoping he might have ideas on how I can get the boat home."

"Your US Coast Guard will have no power here," Jhosep cautioned her.

Silvio offered, "There are not a lot of places to access the internet, although we hear the government is going to allow more cafés next year. Since we are getting more tourists, it is becoming a necessity. You are welcome to use the computer at my office in Havana tomorrow. It will be much more economical for you than finding and dealing with a café in the city. At my office, it will be free. And if you have no luck with your phone, we will loan you Ann's."

"Thank you, that is so good of you."

Jhosep said he would use Ann's car and pick her up in the morning, but Meg said no. He had already done enough. If they could just give her directions and a good time to go, she would find her way. Meg struggled accepting help from strangers, but she didn't have a lot of choices.

Silvio announced almost demandingly, "My father will take you. It's silly. He has nothing to do, and we have a car. Just say yes."

"Yes." Meg's voice hesitantly submitted.

"Well, you know," Silvio said, "you're going to need to have CUCs while you are here. The CUC is the tourist money. You will pay a hefty fee to convert your US dollars, and when you want to change them to the US, you will pay another one. I can change your dollars into CUCs, and when you leave, I can do it all at no fee to you." Meg felt pressured by his offer but embarrassed not to accept, like she didn't trust him.

"I only have a small amount of money with me tonight," Meg said to him when she checked her bag.

"I will come by the marina tomorrow, and we can make the exchange then. I will be very insulted if you don't allow me to do you this favor."

Silvio had a way about him that when he spoke, there was no alternative but to accept. She should have just stood firm and declined his offers, but she didn't.

Meg asked Jhosep how he came to live so far away from the family. Before Jhosep could answer, Silvio chimed in.

"Jhosep doesn't like the politics of Cuba. He participated in the resistance years ago, and after that, the situation became difficult for him, and he left Havana. It is his way." And Silvio smiled at his father as Jhosep confirmed it. "He doesn't believe what we are doing here benefits the people."

Ann questioned, "What are we doing here, Silvio?" Meg could see that tension was building. Juan played with his food, not knowing what to do. Ann stood up and winked at her son, adding a smile. "It's time for dessert. We have dulce de leche cheesecake."

Juan and his grandfather clapped. Meg knew dulce de leche, and she knew cheesecake. But she had never had them combined. It was a homemade recipe by Ann's housemaid, and it tasted rich and creamy and delicious.

Before Meg left, she offered to pay Jhosep for his time, but his expression said "no" when she said it, so she dropped it. When the evening ended, Meg thanked them again. Ann told Meg to call her and let her know her plans, and they all exchanged cell phone numbers. If Meg only could get service.

Meg pulled a brown leather wallet from her bag and took Juan aside.

"Juan." Meg squatted next to him. His attention was all hers. She cupped her hand lightly on his. "You are a hero, Juan, do you know that? You and your grandfather saved my life. Thank you for helping me. This is my husband's wallet. I bought it for his birthday, but his birthday is tomorrow, and I can buy him another when I see him. I want you to have it. This is to thank you for your kindness and for bringing his *Tori's Seacret* to a safe harbor. I know when I tell him, he would want you to have it." Juan turned his head toward his mom and then his dad, seeking permission, and when they gave it, he accepted the wallet with a hug for Meg.

"Thank you; I will never ever forget you. I believe you will find him and the dog. I will pray for you when I say my prayers tonight that it won't be long."

"Thank you, Juan. I believe it too."

Ann and Silvio dropped Meg by the marina. Meg thanked them again for their hospitality. She vowed she would keep in touch and let them know how things worked out. Ann hugged her like an old friend would, and Silvio squeezed her hands in his and assured Meg that she could count on them. Silvio reminded Meg that he would see her the following day. They sat in the car and watched until Meg reached *Tori's Seacret*. She had enjoyed a pleasant visit at their home, and Meg viewed them as good people. Like Jhosep had done earlier, Meg dragged herself into the boat after the long day, and she crawled into her bed. But before she did, she said a prayer, too, that Juan was correct and it wouldn't be long.

Meg woke early the next day. Outside her eyes scanned the marina, arranged like a series of canals with the boats tied alongside the docks port and starboard. It had room for about one hundred fifty vessels. Meg counted them, and 50 percent of them seemed to be there long term. Most were sailboats, and others were transient fishing boats in Havana for a tournament. A group of brightly painted go-fast boats rafted up three deep from the dock came in. There were orange, red, white, and blue. One had a black Darth Vader stealth design, and one had a blue denim paint job with light and dark metallic designs. She didn't know where they came from, but at the speed they traveled, if it was Miami, the ninety mile trip would barely have taken two hours. When they started their engines, they roared and vibrated the docks.

Meg went to meet Jhosep; she locked up and walked to the marina office. She walked past the pool and bathrooms and showers on her way. Outside the office, in the parking lot, he told her she would find a beat-up, blue-and-white plastic lounge chair. Jhosep told Meg to sit there and wait. Over it a sign read, *"Maestro del muelle solo!* Dockmaster only!"

Meg didn't know the meaning and hoped she broke no law because just as Jhosep pulled up, the dockmaster stuck his head out the door and gave her a frown.

Meg hopped in. "Did I do something wrong?"

"No matter." Jhosep smiled.

The Hemingway Marina was located nine miles west of the city of Havana. On their way, Meg stretched her neck down the road when they passed the cutoff to Silvio and Ann's home. Meg found it more picturesque in the morning sun. In a short time in the distance, Meg began to see the outline of the high-rise buildings of the city of Havana. When they got closer, she remembered the things that the teachers had told her, and now she understood what they meant. Out of the car window, Meg saw a war zone of neglected vacant buildings. The streets were lined with pastel-colored buildings with arches and balconies. There were pink and yellow and blues ones, faded to nearly white from weather and time, all in need of a fresh coat of paint.

"They must have been exquisite once," she said to Jhosep; he nodded in agreement as they drove farther into the center of the city.

"Yes, they were. All of Cuba was. Some countries are dealt an unworthy blow, and they can never recover."

"Like Nicaragua. Political pawns. It's sad," Meg agreed with him.

Jhosep pulled up in front of an old multistory, moderately maintained government building. A far cry from the other buildings she saw on the way. Like John and Sharon had said, a place frozen in time. Tom would have liked to see what she saw and be where she had been the last few days. A part of grief described to her by a girlfriend who'd lost her husband: each time she went to share what she saw or something that happened, she had no one to tell. Her man wasn't there.

Jhosep pointed to an outdoor café on the opposite side of the circle. "I'll wait for you over there."

"Hopefully, I won't be long."

"No matter. Take as much time as you want."

Meg needed to show her permit and her passport as well as the security pass that Silvio gave her once inside the doors of the building. It was what you'd expect of a government building—marble floors that needed polishing, tall columns, and lofty ceilings. The counter that said "Information" was unoccupied, but after a few moments, a young woman's voice echoed when she called out Meg's name. The name tag pinned over her left breast said "Philomena." After a brief handshake, Meg followed her up two flights of stairs. Philomena wore one shoe three inches higher than the other, but in spite of it, Philomena maneuvered the climb considerably ahead of Meg. Philomena opened the door to an office big enough to hold a few men and women at desks with computers. She led her in and motioned to one that Meg could use. Next to it, the woman sat down and went to work, not saying another word.

There was an internet browser activated, but not one she recognized. She began to search for an AOL mail site, found it, and entered her address and password. The system moved very slowly, but once in, she brought up her daughter's address and typed an email she wished she could have said in person.

> Carol. I am ok. I am in Cuba on the boat at Hemingway Marina near Havana. There was a storm, then a huge wave. It flipped the boat, and Dad was lost.

When Meg wrote it, it sounded so emotionless, so matter of fact, but that's what it was. That was what had happened.

This is the first chance I've had to email you. I called yesterday, from the marina office, but you didn't answer. I spoke with the commander at the Key West coast guard yesterday. I have no cell service but did meet people here who have helped me. I will recheck email later today if I can from the marina, but their service is spotty and not always available. I am hoping to get my phone working. I will call you when I can. It's been horrible, but I have not given up hope of finding your father.

Love you,

Mom

Meg logged off the email and browsed boating accidents and missing persons in Florida and Key West. She found it. An image of Meg, Tom, and Bitti posing in front of Captain Blinky's pilot boat on the Key West bight. The picture taken by a passing tourist before they left for Mexico that she shared on Facebook.

That night they'd gone for dinner at their favorite Key West steak house. Sitting in the office, she got lost in her thoughts of that evening. Later, Tom had made espresso martinis. She could hear the ice rattle in her head when Tom shook it repeatedly in the shaker, and after that he poured the light-brown, frothy liquid into their glasses. Meg's senses remembered the aroma of the three coffee beans that he sprinkled on top. No one could make them like her Tom. They sat in the cockpit and listened to their favorite Eagles CD. They sang "Ol' 55" over and over till they both dozed off in their chairs

Unfortunately, they hadn't had a lot of those times together, of late. Meg had said things to him before they left home. And without telling him, Meg had gotten tested for the early onset Alzheimer's gene, a thing he never expected of her. She wanted to volunteer to be part of a study. She wanted him to be tested too. But Tom disagreed; he didn't want to know. Meg told him when they were done with the trip, things would be different between them. She would begin to make her own choices. Tom didn't understand this change in her. They had words, and he walked off, angry.

Being on the verge of this long-planned trip, they'd decided they would talk about it later. That was like going to bed mad. Only Tom and Meg were not just going to bed. They were going to sea. Then the accident and no time to clear the air. No time for I'm sorry, for either one of them. Meg remembered setting her phone alarm for the early departure that morning. The date of the article in the *Keynoter* post with their photo was June 29, which was two days after the photograph had been taken. It reported the missing sport fisher, *Tori's Seacret*.

When Meg finished, she came out of the building and walked to where Jhosep sat.

"Would you like a coffee? I am having another." He said it as he rolled up a political newspaper that someone had left at the table. When she looked at him, he looked pale and appeared distraught.

"Yes, I would, thank you."

"Did you find everything you wanted?" he asked her. Meg began to answer him, when she saw Jhosep's expression go blank. His head fell forward hard on the table. Meg jumped from her chair and put her fingers on Jhosep's neck, feeling a pulse. She screamed at the waiter for help. When the ambulance arrived, Jhosep had regained consciousness. He objected to getting in but had to agree. Something was very wrong. Meg got in with him. She needed to call Silvio, but Jhosep didn't carry a cell phone, and hers didn't work.

The hospital in Havana wasn't far. The pretty nurse at the admittance counter said she knew Silvio, and when Meg gave her his card, she called him. Meg waited, feeling helpless, on the edge of the bench in the emergency room, while the doctor attended to Jhosep. She knew the signs of a stroke and felt grateful for the quick response. From what she could see, he didn't have any apparent side effects. The doctor came out to see her. He told her that Jhosep appeared to have come through without any serious problems, but other tests needed to be done.

"Are you his wife?" he asked.

"No, I am a friend. We were having coffee when he collapsed. I used the desk phone, and I called his son."

Two hours later and after they admitted Jhosep, Silvio still hadn't arrived at the hospital. Meg became concerned. She had no money to catch a taxi, and Ann's car was parked downtown by Silvio's office. She wondered why she hadn't seen Silvio at his office earlier.

Meg learned that in Havana, she could make her way without speaking much Spanish. Most of the educated people could speak English, and in the hospital, while it wasn't their first choice, they could speak it.

Meg walked to the information desk.

"Excuse me. English?"

One of the men at the desk responded.

"Yes, I can help you."

"I need to convert US dollars to CUCs. Is there a bank nearby?"

He pointed to the front door and pointed left. "Short walk," he said.

Meg followed his directions. She'd learned from other places that when a person said, "a few blocks," or "a short walk," it could be three miles. After five blocks, still walking, she began to wonder how much farther. All of a sudden, at a corner, a horn blew, and a black car swerved to the curb in front of her. It was Silvio.

"What are you doing here? Did Jhosep abandon you?" He didn't know.

"Oh my goodness, Silvio. Jhosep is at the hospital. He is ok, but he's had a stroke. The hospital called you. I am walking to the bank to change some money for a taxi."

"You don't need a taxi; get in. I'll take you there."

At the hospital, Silvio whisked by the nurse, and he winked at her when he went by. "How's my father?"

"We called you, Silvio." She gave him a flirty smile.

Meg saw Silvio. His behavior toward the nurse. Silvio liked the ladies.

Meg waited another thirty minutes, and when Silvio came out the doors to the waiting area, he dangled the car keys in his hand. "Come on, he'll need to stay a few days. I'll take you to pick up Ann's car. You can follow me to our home, and then I can take you to the marina."

In the car, he talked positively about what the doctor had told him. "We have excellent doctors here in Cuba. Jhosep will be fine."

"You do have excellent doctors; I just didn't know the doctor's skills were sold out to the world. If I spent the time studying, I would want to have more control of where I practiced."

"It's the way it is here, and it has been this way since Castro. Even before."

Meg got in Ann's car, which Jhosep had parked by the café. She followed close behind Silvio. She felt nervous about driving a car in a country where she had no driver's license. When they arrived, Ann was not at home. They didn't tarry. Meg parked Ann's car and hopped in the front seat next to Silvio.

At the marina that afternoon, Meg bought a SIM card for her phone, although it had limited use. The first number she called was Tom's, and when it rang in the drawer next to the sofa, she jumped. That's where he'd left it. She saw a previous call on the screen. But it was her call to his phone from the dockmaster's office the day before.

Then Meg made another call to her daughter. When she called her number, her daughter would answer, but they were disconnected. Then Carol called. They made a successful connection that turned into an emotional dialogue. Carol told her mother that she wanted her to get on a plane and come home. Carol cared little about *Tori's Seacret*. The efforts to find her father had come back negative, and she wanted her mother home. Meg objected. "I plan to get a captain we know to bring the boat home where it needs to be and go search for Dad."

"Where, Mom, to the middle of the ocean?"

Meg became quiet, and her emotions let loose again. Carol's choice of words to her was in poor taste. But their conversation ended amicably after Carol added, "Mom, I know you are doing what you think Dad would want you to do. But Dad isn't here now, and I am asking you to do what's best for you. Should I be flying there?"

"No, No. Carol, I will do the right thing for me. Be patient. I am hurting, and I need to do this."

Afterward, Meg weighed what Carol had said to her. Meg wasn't ready to consider the possibility that Tom had been lost. To Meg, Tom was invincible. She would surely die before him.

Meg sat in the cockpit, thinking more about her day at sea and the evening at Silvio and Ann's home. And after that day's events, now another day would pass. She thought nothing had been accomplished. A lot had been. She'd talked to the coast guard, she'd seen the *Keynoter* article, and she'd spoken with her daughter. People knew she survived.

Were those reasons enough to celebrate? Probably not. But Meg needed a drink. She filled her shaker to the top with ice and measured the golden scotch equal parts with dry vermouth like Tom would have done. Meg shook it so vigorously the drink poured out like a slushy into the glass. Two blue-cheese-stuffed olives dropped in completed the drink. It was the first one Meg had had since the steak house in Key West. She made a double, feeling positive that good things had to follow.

A growling sound stirred in her middle, but dinner could wait. She carried her drink and a plate of cheese and chorizo sausages out to the cockpit. After drink number one, Meg was feeling mellow. After that, reckless, then amorous.

Down the dock came the distinguishable figure of Silvio walking toward her. Meg had hoped he had forgotten about his offer of the money exchange because she had. She wanted to get up and go inside and pretend like she didn't see him. He already had a clear view of her, and Meg knew that it wasn't the right thing to do. So she sat there, and when he approached her smiling, she stood up and invited him aboard.

"Did everything work out for you when you were at my office today? With everything that happened with Jhosep, I forgot to ask you."

"Yes," Meg responded, "I did the research I needed to do and also got a SIM card for my phone. I spoke with my daughter. She wants me to come home."

"Well," Silvio said, "you can understand that. She has to be worried about you. You are a woman alone in a foreign country. And you are vulnerable." Meg didn't know if she liked or agreed with that. Did she come off that way to others? The drink began to speak for her.

"I am not afraid. I am way past that. I have to do what I have to do. I just don't know what that is yet." Meg hesitated and saw that she'd surprised him by her overly confident, defensive remark. He changed the subject.

"From the wine you brought us last night, you have a very nice wine collection aboard."

"It's not me. My husband is the wine connoisseur. But it is starting to run low." For the short time Silvio and Meg had known each other, they spoke easily. She had met men like Silvio before who, with their bedroom eyes and nature, move right in. Practice made perfect for them. Part of Meg wanted to see Ann come around the corner and join them, and part of her didn't. Meg found shame in that part. That was not like her—so she thought.

"Would you like a glass?"

"No, but I will take a glass of cognac or scotch if you have it." Meg said she had both and poured him a scotch on the rocks and made another double for herself. In the cockpit, the two of them sat and talked. Old feelings overwhelmed her, with Silvio next to her relaxed in Tom's chair, sharing a drink with her. And if it were Tom, she would have grabbed his hand. Silvio's conversation continued with more questions.

"So, what do you think of what you have seen of Havana, so far? Did they treat you well at my office?"

"Yes, at the office, the young woman who met me, Philomena, was pleasant. We didn't speak much. And after she got me to a computer, she went to work. Is she your secretary?"

"No, I have a large staff. Sweet Philomena is just one of many."

His answer surprised her. He spoke almost as if he owned them. "I would imagine that your position is an important one. Education is so important in every country. How we educate our youth will affect us all."

"Yes, there is much controversy here in Cuba on that now. As you said, our literacy standing is very high in the world. It is not about how we educate our young but their future afterward. I don't know if I will see it in my lifetime, but change is on the horizon for Cuba."

"Then it's a good time to be young in Cuba. A good future is in store for Juan." Meg raised her glass to Silvio's.

"We are hoping so. Juan is intelligent, and he is a good person. Ann has taught him well."

Meg went on to tell him how it came down when Juan and Jhosep found her off Cape San Antonio and the trip to Havana. She hadn't considered it luck that his father and his son were the ones that saw the flares. Meg rambled on. Now she'd had too much to drink. Silvio cocked his head and gave her a teasing smile as he listened to her recount. Meg tried not to notice, but because of the drink, she couldn't help but smile at him.

"Why don't you stay longer? I would like to take you to see the real Cuba, not just Havana. You should see Trinidad. It is the gem of Cuba."

Meg thought that maybe she read more into his words and his smile. Since meeting him yesterday, she'd felt attracted to him. And now tonight, after all that had happened, she did feel vulnerable. Meg was used to a man in her life, like Silvio, taking control.

Meg had been a loyal wife. She wasn't stupid and knew where things were going. Silvio flattered her. But Tom was the only thing that mattered to her. Silvio finished his scotch; he set his glass on the table, and when he could see that's all there would be, he stood up, stretched his torso, said good night, and went on his way. Meg closed and locked the salon door, and she realized they hadn't talked of exchanging her dollars for CUCs. She had been right; he hadn't come to exchange the dollars. He'd come for more from her.

It bothered her. Why do men do this? Her husband could be clinging to a pallet at sea or even worse. Meg had told herself that there would be no more crying, but contrary to that, Meg realized such disappointment in herself that she cried again that night until she couldn't cry anymore, and then with the influence of drink, she fell asleep.

CHAPTER EIGHT

Fun in the Dominican Republic

With Tom and Bitti aboard and German at the helm and Antonio as his mate, *Moet* continued on its path to the Dominican Republic. Hulia confirmed her flight to meet Mariana and *Moet* in Punta Cana. Mariana made up her mind to make Hulia's visit a good one. Plans to take her to her favorite restaurant—which served pistachio-encrusted grouper for lunch and orange cake for dessert—were made. Afterward, they would rummage through trendy boutiques in Punta Cana and visit the spa for manicures and pedicures while enjoying late-afternoon tea and biscotti.

Mariana had just now turned sixty. Her skin and her body were tight. Except for her hands, which now had become veiny, and her neck, which gave in to gravity, still one couldn't guess her age. Her figure allowed her to wear the current styles worn by forty-year-olds like her daughter. It was the same for Hulia. The two of them turned heads. Both were the same age, but they hardly appeared to be a day over fifty, either one of them.

Aboard *Moet*, there were five of them: Mariana, German, Antonio, Tomas, and of course, Chandon. On the third day, Tomas met Chandon. Antonio had created an area on the port side of the boat for dog walking. He'd used leftover artificial turf from the putting green he'd installed on the top deck. On that day, Chandon smelled her breakfast of bacon and eggs Antonio had cooked for her in the galley and caught the whiff of Tom as she ran past him in the salon. She stopped dead in her tracks, made a sharp U-turn. To get his attention, she smiled, one side of her lip up, then the other, her tail wagging like a high-speed metronome. She turned her head like a dog in a phonograph ad asking, "And where have you been?"

Bending to reach her, Tom scratched her behind her ear. "That's right." She accepted his advance and leaned into it. But when he turned and went off to his job, she sat disappointed.

"Whaaaat?"

During Tom's break time, he went to the cubicle dedicated to the crew's computer. Selecting Google as his search engine and choosing English over Spanish, Tom entered the yacht's name in the browser: *Moet*, Hargrave, motor yacht. A Portuguese company that produced olive oil and honey on the Douro River owned the boat. Photos of their product line and their distributors around the world, and one other link for contacts, were available. No information on the board of directors. The company had been in business for over one hundred years, a small family enterprise that began with bees and olive trees and grew to be a worldwide corporation. On the opening page was a close-up of an older couple outfitted in bibbed jeans. They stood in front of acres of green olive trees. They were Mariana's grandparents, who had raised her. Besides Mariana's lawyer, Hymie, only a few knew that Mariana and her daughter were the last living heirs to the fortune.

Tom took a piece of paper and wrote a list of words in English. These were words he wanted to know in Spanish. He had questions that he might want to ask. Roles he may have played in his life. After he wrote them, he added the Spanish translation and pronunciation to his list. These were words like: *home, husband, wife, father, mother, family, remember, lonely*, and *sadness*. Words he may want to say, to ask. The word *lonely* he knew, but at that point, not for whom or why. *Sadness*, he just felt.

Home = *la casa*
Husband = *so esposa*
Wife = *la esposa*
Father = *el padre*
Mother = *la madre*
Family = *la familia*
Remember = *recorder*

Lonely = solo
Sadness = la tristeza

Tom reread the words, some of which he'd known before. One, now, he would not forget: solo, "lonely." It made sense to him and was easy for him to remember. He folded the paper into a square, slipped it into his top pocket, and returned to his duties. He would be sure to refer to them again in this journey.

Moet's arrival in Hispaniola's waters was silently broadcasted to them by the jagged mountainous coastline. The ominous view made the crew watch in awe from their stations, a land that could have been a setting for the movie, Jurassic Park. For a split second, they expected to hear the prehistoric screams of pterodactyls flying above. But a change in course, bringing them closer to land, brought them to reality.

Like in many other countries Tom had visited, pulling in just anywhere and dropping anchor or throwing a line was not allowed. The government designated ports to clear immigration and customs, and there were only a few. Haiti suffered from poverty and political controversy, and on January 12, 2010, a catastrophic 7.0 earthquake with fifty-two aftershocks killed over three hundred thousand people. The Dominican Republic, in contrast, thrived with the influx of the European and American tourist trade. There were all-inclusive resorts built by corporate entities that lured newlyweds for honeymoons and families for holidays. Still, both were considered third-world countries by some, and precautions were necessary.

For Antonio, it seemed like forever since he'd last set foot on dry land, and there was another ten hours' travel time still between them and Punta Cana on the northeast coast. German recommended to Mariana that they stop and anchor in the bay at Luperón in the Dominican Republic, have dinner, let the crew rest, and continue to Punta Cana the following day.

Luperón lay on the north coast of Hispaniola, just east of the border of Haiti, in the Dominican Republic. Puerto Blanco Bay, a secluded sailboat anchorage and known hurricane hole, offered protection on all sides by thick mangrove trees that grew low and close to the shore. The bay led into a river that continued inland, allowing rising water to flow through. Shoals of sand ran on the left and right of the inlet. At high tide they were not visible, but perilous. The local fishermen marked the channel with batches of homemade buoys made from coconuts. They painted the buoys on the right bright red, and ones on the left Kelly green—hence, red on the captain's right guiding him in, when returning from the sea.

Going ashore for dinner gave Mariana a reason to dress up. She got out a midlength, tiered, yellow-and-orange skirt with a crocheted hem. Mariana topped it off with a beige, off-the-shoulder, ruffled blouse and a pair of high-wedge-heeled, orange espadrilles that were laced up her calf and tied with a bow.

After Antonio dove *Moet*'s anchor to verify it was holding, they lowered the tender and they drove the short distance to the land and tied it at the bar's small dock. They climbed the narrow slab stairway to the top of the precipice. Tomas carried Chandon, and Antonio guided Mariana while she held her skirt up and watched her footing on the steep incline. Built into the base of a kapok tree was Gallo Rojo (Red Rooster) Bar. The enormous tree measured twenty feet in diameter and was over one hundred feet tall. It branched out so far that its leaves formed an umbrella, keeping patrons cool in the heat and dry in the rain. The staff carved images in dried-out coconuts using scallop shells for ears and hung them from the branches, each one uglier than the last. After sunset, for ambiance, they lit candles in the low-hanging heads.

From the restaurant, they watched over *Moet*, moored in the bay with its shiny new lights. A few other boats shared the bay. Daylight waned. A red sunset behind tall palms and the Hispaniola pine forest outlined their view of the border between Haiti and the Dominican Republic.

The modest restaurant had an excellent local menu and live music at night. The bamboo-reed bar sold alcohol. Other patrons sat at square tables and watched the crew of *Moet* when they filed in. *Moet*'s owner and crew sat together, and Mariana treated them as equals. They had deep-fried whole yellowtail snapper at round, wooden picnic tables, eating from paper plates and palm-weaved place mats. A generous portion of fried bananas and yellow curry rice accompanied the fish. Mariana wished they could duplicate the snapper recipe aboard *Moet*. She teased Tom about it after he said that he would like to take a turn in the galley.

The guys shared a pitcher of beer, and Mariana drank a bottle of Pinot Gris that they'd brought in a bag with them from *Moet*'s cellar. The bartender took their orders, and when he made small talk about where they had been and where to next, Antonio began to tell him, but German cut him off. German didn't like to share plans with people he didn't know, and he quickly changed the subject. German asked if they needed to check in at the main pier, and the bartender, whose name was Jesus, said, "Yes, with the commandant." So they agreed between them that in the morning, Antonio would go over early to take care of customs and immigration, not mentioning Tomas's name. No one cared or hassled boaters at Puerto Blanco.

After dinner, Mariana asked Jesus if he could make Strawberries Romanoff, a fresh strawberry dessert with ice cream and liqueur. The waiter apologized, but Tom knew the recipe. Jesus spoke English, and Tom asked if he had the ingredients. He needed ice cream, strawberries, whipped cream, and a liqueur.

"Yes, I have all that." He lined up the liqueur, a box of strawberries with stems, and a can of whipped cream in front of Tom on the bar and pointed to a room off the galley.

"There's vanilla ice cream in that freezer. It's probably hard as a rock."

Tom took over behind the bar. First, he spooned out the ice cream in a large bowl and left it out in the warm air to melt a little. When the strawberries were cleaned and sliced in bite-size pieces, he folded the whipped cream and softened ice cream together and spooned it all into large goblets meant for colossal margaritas. As a finishing touch, he added a generous portion of liqueur to each glass. Before he served them, he gave one to Jesus. Mariana and her crew dipped their spoons in the creamy vanilla strawberry blend. When each tasted the kick from the Grand Marnier, they closed their eyes and smiled. Jesus searched for a piece of paper for Tom to jot down the recipe. Tom wrote out the recipe: "For Jesus, Tomas's Strawberries Romanoff," and dated it Tuesday, July 3.

During dessert, a wrinkled old man arrived wearing a straw cowboy hat with a crocodile band. He carried a ukulele, and when Jesus gave him a beer, he began to play. Having had more than her share of the wine, Mariana's body gyrated with the tempo of the beat. German rolled his eyes, sending a message to Antonio and then over to Tomas. Both Antonio and German knew that one of them had to dance with Mariana. They'd both taken their turn in the past. Antonio stepped on his cigarette and took his turn first. Antonio liked both jazz and hip-hop, and he dipped in and out, side to side, and then did the splits on the floor. Mariana stood with her hands on her hips, grinning at him. She grabbed her skirt and waved it around while she clicked her heels on the concrete floor and did the two-step matador dance to compete with his steps. When they were done, they both bowed, and their audience applauded.

Tom liked to dance. He always did. All men knew that all their wives wished they had married a man that danced. They wanted a man that could take their hand and lead them over the dance floor like a lady. Even though they loved their men, they wished theirs could dance. Tomas took Mariana on the floor next to their table, and they danced in a way that she had not danced in a while. Even though he stepped aside, German hid envious eyes. Her hair smelled sweet as a gardenia, and when he held her close, Mariana responded. He held her longer and closer than he should have, and Mariana liked it.

After two more dances and before they boarded the tender, Tom and Mariana walked Chandon along the sandy shore of the bay. The smell of smoke hung in the air. Crushed shells that bled in from the ocean were all over the beach, with the variety redesigned every day with the movement of the tides. A few couples off sailboats sat on large pieces of driftwood and enjoyed the peaceful night. Two American men who resembled each other built a small fire from the wood and sat and drank beers from the bar. One played the banjo and sang a little John Denver, about the Rocky Mountains that were high. And when Tom observed their demeanor, he smiled and thought for sure the two brothers were in fact high on something.

Tom had a sense of yesterday and someplace else, but Tomas didn't understand why. He thought of the list of words he had just made, and he thought about the word *la familia*, family. He wondered. Did he have one? One brother held out his blue vein-ridden hand, and Chandon smelled it, for that one specific scent. She searched for only one. But not there, so she moved on. The other brother rubbed her ear, and she rewarded him with a smile, one lip up, then the other. Afterward, the two brothers commented to themselves on what an odd couple Mariana and Tom were. He was an American, all scarred and sunburned and peeling, and she one fancy lady with a deep, thick kind of Latin accent.

They climbed aboard *Bubbles* and returned at slow speed to *Moet*. The crew secured it at the gangplank as the four of them settled in for the night. Tomas sat on the stern on a comfy lounger, and Chandon climbed up next to him. The little dog sensed old times. She crawled up his chest and licked his jaw again and again with her sandpaper tongue until he had to push her down and away. The dog knew his head wasn't right, and he needed a friend.

They left Luperón very early in the morning, and German had scheduled to arrive in Punta Cana late that night. He alerted the dockmaster. *Moet*'s bow crashed in the wind and the waves. It made the trip longer. The ominous black and green mountainous terrain of the northern Dominican Republic rose up at their starboard side. No houses or structures dotted them. Mahogany trees grew tall, and huge boulders formed cliffs, and a mist hung among them. German set a heading to keep *Moet* far offshore to avoid plowing into tree stumps that fell down the gradient and floated in the water after the rains. They caused chaos for unaware boaters.

Eighty miles off the port side were the shoals of the Silver Bank. Tourists visited the bank in the winter months and lived aboard dive boats and swam with humpback whales that migrated there. The divers would sign on for weeks at a time and enjoy the adventure.

Moet passed Puerto Plata and the Dominican World Resort. It caused a déjà vu moment for Tom. He knew he had been there before. A marina, casino, and a live sea creature exhibit. A top-rated destination with the local people and tourists. An architect had created a unique building with mosaic tiles laid on the side of the building and the walkways duplicating waves of water with playful dolphins swimming on them. Unfortunately, the marina attached to it created a washtub for yachts in the winter when the north winds blew. When Tom had been there before, it lacked flow-through of water built into its design. The waves came in and then ricocheted against the sea walls of the marina. Once a boat got into the marina, it couldn't get out until the north wind subsided. That could be a long time. It didn't take long for the news to spread and for captains to steer their vessels to other ports. Word had it that a jetty had been added to shield the inlet from the wind and waves, but it could not be seen as they motored by.

Mariana loved to play games. She had a puzzle going in *Moet*'s game room. When she had guests, they always stopped in to find a piece that fit. Even the crew would sneak in to fit a piece to move it along when they walked by. Most of her puzzles were purchased in Europe. She enjoyed putting together photography puzzles of breathtaking places she had been. She'd worked days on one of the coastal city of Porto, where she'd lived many years of her life. Tom came in and sat next to her to get a clear view of her progress. They both sat silently, studying the colors of the landscape of the city. Mariana smiled at him. All at once, they both grabbed for the same piece, and they laughed as she let him have it, and he placed it in its spot. She liked him, and Tom liked her too.

The Samaná Peninsula east of Puerto Plata held the next port of entry. At the mouth, there were huge tankers and freighters transporting supplies anchored and waiting for entry. There were commercial fishing boats and many permanently moored sailboats with liveaboards. At night you could see their anchor lights listing from their masts. Primarily this was where the service people lived. Tom remembered Samaná a lively, busy city, and for the most part, the people were pleasant, and crime wasn't bad. But yachts like *Moet* continued past Samaná and east to the newer tourist area of Punta Cana. Splendid resorts and marinas welcomed their vessels and their money. It took a full day to travel from Luperón to Punta Cana.

Tomas had begun doing a little cooking in the galley on *Moet*. He had prepared lunch, and that night he planned his first special dinner. They had duck breast in the freezer. He had a recipe of wild rice and shiitake mushrooms sautéed with scallions. He used carrots, onions, and broth and created a velvety sauce for the duck. The aroma of the meal filled *Moet*. Mariana and Chandon sniffed it from her cabin.

Tomas chose a bottle of Pinot Noir to accompany the meal. They had a varied selection onboard. Mariana showed up on deck, dressed in black pants that flowed in front of her when she walked and a sparkly gold blouse. Her earrings hung from her lobes and sparkled like diamonds, and Tomas assumed that they were. He smelled the soft cork that came out of the bottle with ease and poured a little in a glass for Mariana to taste. He passed her the glass, and when her lips tasted the Pinot, she gave the nod to him. None of this pairing could have been done by her crew.

German and Antonio had left the boat for dinner and beers. Mariana disliked eating alone, so she sat Chandon on the chair close up next to her. Not accustomed to sitting at a table, Bitti stretched her neck tall so her nose could take in the smells. She had smelled this meal before but had never been invited to dinner. Mariana folded her napkin on her lap and motioned Tomas to take the chair at the table near Chandon. He smiled, said *gracias*, poured himself a glass of wine, and sat down. Not the place for a crewmember to be, but he had no underhanded motives and did not contemplate his actions to be out of line.

He asked her, "Did you enjoy your meal?" Of course, he knew, she'd polished her plate clean.

"*Bueno, bueno,*" she said, in her thick, smoky voice. "You are an excellent chef. You must have been a chef in your previous life."

Tomas listened, but no answers popped into his mind. He chose the perfect wine, and he saw she appreciated his understanding of fine things. He knew deep inside that he had appreciated excellence. But Tom had a monetary limit and was not acclimated to her bottomless pit kind of living.

She played her favorite music, and a glorious breeze blew through the boat. Mariana leaned in and stretched across the table to him. Tomas found no embarrassment at the moment, and things might have escalated, but he had emptied his glass, and he could hear German and Antonio talking as they climbed aboard.

He smiled and commented, "Bueno vino, gracias. Buenos notches." He thought he'd said, "Good wine, thank you, and good night," but she had a long face, so he didn't know for sure. He did know that sometimes an *a* or an *s* on the end of a Spanish word can change the whole meaning. She appeared disappointed. But, inside his heart, he knew he had a love, and it was not she.

On his way to his cabin, German stole a quick peek into the dining room as he walked by. The two empty glasses of wine on the table said what he'd guessed. Tomas had moved in.

Tomas went to his cabin and undressed. The air conditioning in his cabin had a hard time keeping him cool. He stood in a lukewarm shower, the water running through his hair, his eyes closed, with thoughts of his day. He had always done his best thinking in there. He wanted to linger longer with the refreshing stream on his body. He knew even on a yacht this large, he needed to conserve water. He rotated the handle to the off position and grabbed a towel that smelled fragrant like a woman's perfume. It had a large scripted *M* engraved on it in metallic gold threads. He wondered, The *M* for *Moet* or Mariana?

Tomas quickly dried himself with it and sat at the foot of his bunk. He poured a small glass of scotch from a bottle that Antonio had given him and swallowed it quickly. Then Tomas poured another. His lids closed, and he fell dead to the world.

A memory jolted Tomas, and Tom let out a scream. He fell hard on the cabin floor and woke up. He could see the tuna door swinging open in the cockpit of a boat named *Tori* something as it drifted away from him in rough water. Tom had remembered. Shaking his head, he craved to remember more, an explanation of what happened to him the days before *Moet* found him. But that's all. He was dog tired and slept until 5:00 a.m.

Morning came too early for *Moet*'s new chef. The previous day's travel on the open sea made him tired. He was busy in the galley pulling eggs and bacon out of the refrigerator. He planned to scramble the eggs with thyme, fry up bacon and potatoes, and defrost cinnamon bread for toast. The sun had not come up, and when his finger switched the light on in the galley, Tomas could see into the salon and the dining area.

Mariana lay sleeping on the sofa. As he got closer, he saw that an empty bottle of wine and a plastic bottle of purple hearts lay next to her. He pitied her in her long white bedgown that belonged to a bride. Her cleavage bulged up to her neckline. Lying there, she innocently tempted him. He quickly poured a large cup of hot coffee and sat next to her. She took shallow breaths. He shook her gently. When he did, and she came around, she gestured confusion and embarrassment and wiped her black, made-up eyes with the base of her palms. When Mariana acted alert and could stand up, he guided her into her cabin and to her bed. She followed orders, although when Tomas turned to leave, she grabbed his hand and kissed it. Tomas's body responded. He wanted to stay, but Tom would not take advantage of an overserved, pill-popping woman. He began to know a little more about Mariana, the woman who had saved his life.

Tom continued to arrange his ingredients on the counter for breakfast, got the frying pans out on the stove, and then waited for sounds of German and Antonio. Nothing like the smell of applewood bacon frying up on the cooktop. He cooked for all of them that morning. They all liked him much better as a chef than as a deckhand. They didn't need him to speak the language; they just wanted him to keep on cooking. Today Hulia would arrive and with her a change of pace for everyone on motor yacht *Moet*. They had a guest coming aboard to entertain.

Lovely Hulia arrived later with an entourage carrying her bags and gifts and a cat named Fiona. Both she and the cat were adorned with diamonds and gold, including the gem-studded collar around Fiona's neck. The cat had a "Don't bug me; where's my litter box?" expression on her face after her long trip. Mariana and Hulia hugged and laughed and hugged more, as Fiona tried to squeeze out between them and onto the floor. When Fiona's paw stepped on Bitti's turf, Bitti debated whether there was room for the two of them.

"And who is this little fluff ball? How long has she been with you?" Hulia asked Mariana.

"This is Chandon, Hulie." And Mariana swallowed deep and glanced away when she said it. Hulia read a lie on her friend's face. Then Mariana changed the subject.

"Look at you, Hulie, you are still so thin. How do you do it with all the sweet pastries you eat?"

"Aw, girlfriend, you are too kind. You know I am on the go all the time. I really don't eat that much." Hulia could eat everything and never gain a pound. After they finished a meal, the food remained all scattered around the edges of her plate. Hulia had long, slender arms with fingers that wrapped around the neck of a martini glass with ease. Her torso was not unlike a giraffe's, whereas Mariana had a curvy, fully bodied figure.

Mariana and Hulia knew each other from youth and then from their time studying at the University of Mexico City. They'd stood in each other's weddings, which were both over, and they knew each other's secrets.

Hulia fixed her hair in a tight bun at the top of her head. She usually unpinned it and let the long golden ponytail hang down like *I Dream of Jeannie.* Hulia's cheekbones were high and garnished with color. Her eyebrows were dark brown, well defined, and expressive when she spoke. Hulia arrived in a gold-and-red tunic with matching gold silk pants. Gold flats and simple solid gold beads completed her ensemble. She'd had a lot of work done on her and spent her free time traveling, shopping, and dining. She visited the spa, played tennis, and golfed.

Hulia's life once included family. Her husband, Carlo, had been a Colombian politician, and they had two daughters and a son. During the mid nineties, the five of them had been aboard American Airlines flight 965, originating in Miami and destined for Colombia, when the plane went down. There were four survivors among the 157 on board, and Hulia was one of them. She was thirty-seven at that time, and most of the years after that were a blur filled with surgical repairs from the accident and great sadness. She lived those years at her parents' home in Bogotá, questioning life and her god. These days, she lugged her grief around in her heart, and she allowed a little grief to show now and then, but there had become room for happiness with friends and her business.

Hulia spoke loud and was always ready to party. Hulia teased her friend. "You have FOMAP, fear of missing a party, Mariana."

And Mariana teased her friend back. "No, No, Hulie, you have one over me. You have FOMA, fear of missing anything."

Then they would push at each other like two teenage girls and laugh.

Mariana called in the crew to greet Hulia—German and Antonio, whom Hulia already knew from past visits, and now *Moet*'s new chef, Tomas. Hulia arched one of her darkly sculptured eyebrows when she saw him and glanced over at Mariana. The eyebrow thing was a talent of hers. It would make Mariana laugh. She knew what Hulia thought. American women loved

Latin men, and this Latin woman loved American men. She shook hands with them all, and when Tomas added *no Española*, she smiled. "Better yet."

Mariana walked with Hulia to her cabin. It had been redecorated since her last visit. The bed was a king size, and the white bedspread had an intricate detail of gold thread stitching that created a pattern of whimsical mermaids with voluptuous breasts and long, dark-brown hair. Their faces were white with rosy red cheeks, and each had a crown of shells on her head. A fluffy pink chair was slid in at a white lacquered dressing table. Over the table, Mariana hung an oval mirror framed in seashells that she had collected on beaches. The bathroom, bathtub, and shower were generous in size for a yacht and were adorned with white marble floors and mirrored ceilings.

Hulia had many lovely things, and she found this cabin charming and comfortable. After the long flight from Miami, Fiona's mewing and scratching in her kennel drove Hulia nutty. A man next to her had kept climbing over her, in and out to the bathroom. She'd tried to read and then sleep, but between the man and the cat, it couldn't happen. Her cabin offered her a perfect retreat.

Hulia changed into fresh clothing and joined Mariana up top to see what the plans were for her stay. Hymie, Mariana's attorney, had asked Hulia to report back to him. Hymie spent a great deal of his time booking hours to check up on Mariana. He didn't consider it spying. Since Hulia was visiting her, why not? Whatever Mariana planned, Hulia loved any time they spent together.

Hulia's view from port-side deck showcased the inlet and beyond it the juncture of the Atlantic Ocean and the Caribbean Sea. Further, in the same direction, Hulia could see a stretch of beach with barely a footprint. The marina resort, condominiums, shops, and restaurants stood at the forefront, while the tennis club and golf courses extended to the south end of the development. Long fairways and manicured greens were accented by plantings of mondo grass around each sand trap. Best of all, the giant Canary Island date palms stretched out royally for as far as she could see.

After lunch, Mariana had ordered massage therapists from the resort. Antonio set up two massage tables on the top deck in the shade. A nice breeze blew up there. Hulia loved her idea.

For lunch, Tomas made a clear duck broth from the bones of that week's duck and a romaine chopped salad with large shavings of red cow parmesan cheese, hard-boiled eggs, avocados, candied walnuts, and a freshly made, poppy seed dressing. Additionally, he served a repeat of that superb Pinot Noir that he'd found in the wine cellar down a winding staircase under the galley. Tom used the computer to write his menu. He chose to translate it and print it in Spanish. He even added pictures of tropical flowers and glasses of wine. At the top he wrote, "Lunch on *Moet*, Punta Cana, Dominican Republic, Hispaniola, July 5, 2018."

Mariana and Hulia chatted through lunch about life. Mariana updated Hulia about her daughter, Elena, thirty-five, still living in Mexico City, teaching political science at the university.

Hulia inquired, "How is Elena? Is she still planning to come for the events in Saint Bart?"

"The last we talked, which has been a while now, she said yes."

Elena associated with political types and kept her life private from her mother. Mariana had learned to keep her opinions to herself.

Years after Hulia's family's death, Hulia had become an American citizen, lived in Miami Beach, and opened a successful boutique on Washington Avenue.

"How is your store doing?" Mariana asked her. "I hoped you would bring me samples of new styles. I'd order a dress or two."

Hulia's store, open by appointment only, had the hottest fashions. It drew the young Latin women and a few men to her door seeking the trending styles. Like Hulia, all were as skinny as toothpicks.

Hulia had no current love interests. She kept busy with travel and buying inventories in Europe and New York. She loved her business, and even though she had no education or training as a buyer, it came natural to her.

"Yes, I did. Mar, you know I would bring things for you to see. I know what you like. After lunch, I'll unpack them and hang them up for you to see. These pants I have on were in my last order, and they are so comfortable." When you are skinny, everything is comfortable, Mariana thought.

Their conversation continued on, and the massage therapists arrived late, but the ladies didn't care. They went upstairs to the tables and disrobed.

Before going, Mariana asked Tomas to open another bottle of wine—this time, something fresh and light and fruity—and to bring it up. He didn't know how, but more and more, he and Mariana were finding ways to communicate. She seemed to like everything he did.

This time, Tomas picked a Santa Margarita Pinot Grigio. He recognized it by its label, and he also knew without tasting that it would be delicious. He usually drank it when *she* made veal Française for him. She'd done it for his birthday. His birthday. Tom thought he'd just had one. It was a meal that melted in his mouth, and the cheesy, buttery fettuccini noodles were irresistible to him. When Tom said *she*, a woman's name almost rolled off his tongue. He thought it began with an *M*, like Mariana. He stopped. He pulled his list from his back pocket and read the word, *la esposa*, wife. But the moment and memory were gone as quickly as they had come, and Tomas had a job to do.

Tomas continued on and arranged red seedless grapes and aged cheddar on a bright yellow-and-blue Talavera platter from Puebla, Mexico. Mariana had flown there years ago to have a complete set of dishes made just for her. She'd sat with the craftsman and chosen her colors and designs that were to be distinctive to her. And each piece said so.

How do two women drink wine while getting a massage? With plastic straws, of course. Tomas poured the wine into frosty, insulted-plastic wine glasses and propped them up on a bench under the girls' faces. They giggled when he arrived, and Hulia called out to him.

"Oh, pool boy!" Tomas didn't understand, of course, but he laughed, as both of them were already tipsy from the Pinot Noir at lunch. Two naked women face down on massage tables with *Moet* towels draped over their backsides drinking wine from plastic straws. He didn't remember stuff, but he knew this was not where he came from. Tabby-colored Fiona stealthily wound herself between his feet, arching and rubbing her body on him and squinting up at him with a coquettish grin, like she knew what the girls were laughing about. She stood prone to pounce, and Bitti, who had grown very fluffy now for lack of grooming, sat in the corner wondering if Fiona had moved in for the long haul. When the massages were over, Mariana and Hulia disappeared into their cabins, giddy and tired from the wine and the manipulation of experienced masseurs.

Tomas made it part of his daily routine and checked the web for news in the United States. Chandon jumped up next to him like she had done early mornings at home in the Keys. They would sit by the pool and drink coffee and watch the pelicans perched on the top of each wood piling that supported the dock behind their home. They crouched low with their beaks buried into the feathers on their wings. Then suddenly, like clockwork, they would each take flight and circle in a *V* formation. A couple would break off at the site of a fish and do a high-speed dive straight in for the catch. Bitti would raise her ears in response to the rhythmic squeals of osprey on man-made perches next to their home. Bitti knew what all living creatures knew. It was nature, and it was the season.

Tomas thought a lot about that. In fact, both he and the boss lady did. Mariana didn't speak a great deal of English, but Tomas had learned that she understood a lot. He also knew something would bring them together, and then he would have to make a decision on how far he could let it go. Tom wouldn't take advantage for sex.

Everyone rose early on *Moet* the following morning. German worked on his course for Puerto Rico. Antonio changed fuel filters while doing his laundry. Tomas cleaned the galley while preparing breakfast. Not his specialty, since he rarely ate it, so he chose what he thought Mariana and Hulia would enjoy. He began with mimosas, without the juice—that is, all champagne in a fancy stemmed glass. Why bother with orange juice watered down with champagne? Why not just go straight to the champagne? Mariana's favorite was Veuve Clicquot. They had a case in the cellar. Tom remembered his wife liked Veuve Clicquot. Tomas dropped a raspberry in each glass and watched it as it fizzled and sank to the bottom and carried it out to the girls on a round bamboo tray on his shoulder. Again he remembered, only this time, he remembered the word *wife*. So he had a *wife*.

"I want a mimosa without the mimosa," Meg would say to the waiter. And then they would laugh. Every day now, a few more memories popped into his head, along with emptiness and guilt. But he still couldn't put a face to the memories or comprehend her situation.

Mariana and Hulia took their champagne and moved out to the deck where they could see the boats in the harbor. Beautiful yachts of all sizes were coming and going. Most of the hulls were white, and some were navy blue. After those yachts satisfied customs, a crew member lowered the yellow quarantine flag; they replaced it with the Dominican Republic flag opposite their home country pennant.

Tomas brought out fruit, warm croissants, butter and preserves, and coffee. Mariana and Hulia were making it a day of shopping and lunch, and then a ride into the mountains, before returning to the boat for dinner. On the following day, their itinerary would take them to the south coast of Puerto Rico, to Ponce, once the capital of the south region of the country.

Before the two women left for the day, Mariana called German.

"You need to speak to the dockmaster's office about hiring a cleaning person to join the crew."

"Ok, I'll take care of that now. How long do you want someone?"

"Maybe three months. See if they can recommend someone flexible; you can fly them back here when we get to Tobago." But then Mariana warned him, "No *putas*. Last time you hired a cleaning person, we ended up with a cleaning *puta*, and she ended up such a distraction. German smiled at her and shook his head, because he knew better, and he walked away, repeating under his breath, "No putas, no putas." Mariana smiled too. The marina office helped facilitate employment opportunities, usually matching available jobs to people they knew and recommended.

While the ladies were out for the day, Tomas took Chandon and went to the local market that supplied all the yachts with food and general supplies. His black, two-wheeled dock cart became overloaded with wines, bread, canned goods, onions, garlic, shallots, and meat and fish. The dog sat on top. The market offered a large selection of fresh herbs planted in pots. He liked picking off sprigs of fresh thyme, basil leaves, and parsley while he cooked. And there was nothing like the aroma of fresh basil served on slices of fresh buffalo mozzarella with homegrown tomatoes from locals' gardens. He would serve that as his first course and then make a fillet of beef with gorgonzola sauce, brussels sprouts, and scalloped potatoes. At the bakery, Tomas bought fresh bread and a variety of cheesecakes. Each slice had a different flavor. There were chocolate, lemon, chocolate chip, blueberry, and raspberry. He settled up, signing his name on *Moet*'s account.

Tomas stopped at a school bus parked on the corner of the intersection. Instead of children, each row of seats had baskets of fresh flowers for sale. They were hanging out the windows, creating a sidewalk display. Walking up the steps to the bus, he was overwhelmed by the smells and the colors. Inside, a woman in a red babushka waved Tomas in to consider buying some. Her school-aged daughter did the negotiating. He went away with arrangements of bird of paradise flowers and baby's breath that she suggested for the salon and the dining table and roses for each of the ladies' cabins. A sweet, strong fragrance filled his nose when Tomas took a sniff of the roses. Unlike many flowers, whose growers sacrificed smell to produce large and abundant blooms, these roses had been grown wild. He paid for them in cash and tipped them to deliver them to *Moet*. Tomas also stopped at the crew store and picked out two white lightweight chef's shirts and checkered pants. He enjoyed a good time in his new role, spending Mariana's money. Something Tom wouldn't normally do.

German called ahead to Club de Nautica, a private yacht club in Ponce. After Hurricane Irma, the club and surrounding anchorages had been cleared of debris and sunken boats. The long dock that would accommodate *Moet* still remained under repair, and the dockmaster recommended they drop anchor in the harbor. As captain, German made dinner reservations for Mariana and Hulia at the club the first night. It fulfilled the obligation to patronize a club that offered a transient yacht access to its private facility. The dockmaster helped with docking and many times stayed late when *Moet* arrived after dark. German bought a box of Cuban cigars for him in the Dominican Republic. You couldn't come by them in Puerto Rico. His name was Robal Alvarez, a young fellow for that position at the prestigious club, and German, who had few friends, liked him.

After their day roaming Punta Cana, Mariana and Hulia returned to the boat in the late afternoon. All of Tomas's purchases were already delivered and stowed away. When Hulia walked into her cabin, she hardly had the door open when she smelled the flowers.

What a nice gesture of Mariana to remember she loved yellow roses. Hulia came out from her cabin and hugged Mariana.

"Thank you; you are so sweet, girlfriend."

Mariana hadn't a clue what Hulia meant until she went into her own cabin and found the bouquet of red ones. This was not the deed of Antonio, and certainly not of German. Mariana smiled to herself.

Tomas has added a nice spark to life aboard *Moet*. The roses made Mariana pleased that she'd bought a gift for him while shopping with Hulia. It was probably inappropriate, but she didn't care.

That evening was French martini night aboard *Moet* at Hulia's request. Tomas didn't know if he knew the recipe, but Hulia did. He got a big, juicy, fresh pineapple out of the refrigerator, juiced it in the blender, and opened a bottle of Tito's vodka and Chambord raspberry liqueur. He poured the mixture in a tall carafe, mixed it up, and took a little on his finger to taste.

"Ooh-la-la! It is a lady's drink," Tomas chuckled. "It is delicious."

Tomas took two long-stemmed, blue crystal martini glasses from the freezer and poured a drink for each of the girls. He poured a little in a red solo cup for himself.

After two of those, both girls were twittering about and reliving their day. In the meantime, Tomas plated the meal. The beef came out of the oven, cooked medium rare. After he tasted the sauce, he poured the creamy gorgonzola concoction in a wavy design around the slices of meat. It had a natural nutty flavor. The brussels sprouts he bought were mild and not bitter, and the scalloped potatoes were the perfect blend of cream and cheese that he had hoped for. He proudly presented the plates. He garnished each one with a little purple edible flower that he had gotten at the school bus that day. Tomas puffed up when they oohed and aahed.

"This is too beautiful to eat, Mariana." Hulia smiled. "I need to take a photo of this." Hulia couldn't help but lick the leftover sauce on her plate with her fingers. After they finished, Tomas served them a delicate green salad for digestion that he'd learned by eating in French bistros in Chicago. Then Tomas announced dessert, the only thing he hadn't created, the cheesecake from the bakery. He added fresh raspberries in a vanilla sauce. Both women stood up and left the table.

"Later, later," Hulia said as she waved her arm and shook her head.

The girls had talked earlier about going up to the hot tub after dinner and sipping a woody port Mariana had in her cabinet. Port, which is a fortified wine, went a long way. This one made in Portugal was one of her best.

Once up top, Mariana slipped out of her dress and wrapped her body in a soft camel-colored robe. In her world, nothing could compete with cashmere. It was considered the fabric of queens; she couldn't imagine that any woman had never experienced the pleasure to have cashmere next to her skin. Hulia joined her, clad in a colorful Versace bikini. She wore it fabulously. They watched over the rail to an arched, flower-covered walkway where a lovely young bride with a plunging-back wedding dress and a bouffant veil paraded with a bouquet of white lilies. The rabbi and the groom waited in the chuppah set up near the water. He greeted her with longing eyes. There were words and music, and when the rabbi pronounced them husband and wife, the groom literally swept her off her feet when he kissed her. Mariana and Hulia watched silently with thoughts of days gone by. Hulia still longed for Carlo. Mariana daydreamed of Tomas.

Mariana resentfully changed the subject, called on the speaker, and asked Tomas to bring up the port. He appeared shortly with two small glasses and the bottle of port wrapped in a white mink pouch that Mariana had made to hold her bottles of port and cordials.

"We want to savor this; bring our dessert in a little while."

He nodded and understood.

Thirty minutes passed, and after sipping the fantastic offering, Mariana poured another for herself. Hulia climbed out of the tub. The drinks and the food and the hot water made her nauseous.

"Wait, Hulie, are you pooping out on me already? It's still early."

"Mariana, it's been a wonderful day, but this tub is too small for all of us."

"What does that mean?" Mariana took her comment as odd. But Hulia knew her friend all too well. Hulia said nothing and continued walking down the companionway to her cabin, dripping and bumping against the walls with Fiona following lazily behind her.

Mariana called out her pet name again. "Hulie." And then Mariana blew her the raspberries, closed her eyes, and rested on the pillow in the tub.

When Tomas showed up with their dessert, it surprised him to see Mariana in the hot tub and no one else on the deck. When Mariana opened her eyes, Tomas reached forward to give her the plate. Mariana stood straight up, paused, and pulled him forward into the hot, bubbling tub. In he went, in his new chef's shirt and checkered pants. His fingers grabbed the first body part he found in his fall. Her bodacious tatas. Mariana wound her legs around him, and she kissed him square on his mouth, tongue and all.

No interpretation required, she had seduced him, and Tomas surrendered.

The next morning Mariana and Hulia woke up to the hum of *Moet*'s engines. They were en route to Puerto Rico. Mariana heard a rat tap rap on her cabin door, and she called out to answer. After another quiet knock, a woman, who looked like a teenage girl to Mariana, peeked into the room. She put a tray with coffee and a croissant and butter on the table, smiled, then left. Mariana had just met Angeli, their newly hired housekeeper. She came recommended by Antonio. She was not too pretty and was badly in need of a job. He said she knew how to do her job and stay out of the way.

Mariana's overindulgence the previous night—French martinis, delicious food and wine, and lastly, the port—left her at a loss that morning. She didn't remember seeing Hulia go off to bed; she only remembered being in the tub naked and then feeling the warmth of a man's body in hers. The pillows on the other side of her bed were slept on, and when she pulled one close to her, she smelled Tomas. She hadn't given him the gift she'd bought for him yesterday. It still lay in the box next to her bed. *Moet* was a large yacht, as yachts go, but not so large that German and the others hadn't seen what went on.

Understandably, Tomas felt good that morning. He moved around the galley, a bit arrogant and cocky, putting together fruit and cereal for Hulia. The smell of freshly brewed coffee filled the boat. He liked his position as the head chef aboard *Moet*. He belonged, and after last night, at least he could be sure he was sexually attracted to women.

The ride to Ponce through the Mona Passage took five and a half hours from inlet to inlet. It wasn't uncommon because of the current and the depths; near the Puerto Rican trench, big seas could plague the one-hundred-mile distance. Thankfully for Mariana and her hangover, it was calm. She did quiet things, drank Bloody Marys with a raw egg in a tall glass, and wore her bathrobe by the pool until noon. Mariana, Hulia, and Antonio played mah-jongg. To be a crew member, you had to learn about the Dots and the Cracks, the Bams and the Flowers. They could be compared to the suits in a deck of cards. Antonio became an expert and liked the competition, although his thick fingers struggled to turn the tiles. He complained the tiles were too small. When he discarded a Flower, he stuttered with the *F*—"Fa-fa-fa-fa"—and it embarrassed him. Mariana put her finger up to slow him down, then made him say it over and over slowly until he got it right. "Fa-fa-fa-flower." Antonio smiled tensely when she corrected him in front of Hulia, but in spite of it, he did want to become better.

Mariana's set of tiles came from the old country, where they carved them from bone. It had been her grandmother's set, and like everything else her family owned, it had become hers. Still, the quality set didn't bring her much luck when playing Hulia. Hulia anticipated the tiles that Mariana would play, and she moved fast, choosing and discarding tiles and setting her strategy to say, "mah-jongg." They laughed and screamed, and in the end, Mariana said she had let Hulia win. Hulia punched her in her arm in jest.

Afterward, they worked out in the gymnasium, and then they rested. Mariana and Hulia were dining at the yacht club that night, so after making the girls a light lunch, Tomas had little left to do in the galley. When Mariana rang Tomas's phone from her cabin, he had no excuse but to join her there.

Moet arrived at the inlet. German radioed the dockmaster. An old sailboat ahead of them named *Blo Job* struggled with navigational problems. The twenty-horse engine on the stern choked. The sails weren't offering any help. Following procedure, German gave one blast of his horn to alert the captain he intended to pass. As they did, the bare-chested captain leaned over from behind his large, wood steering wheel. The white-haired sail boater flipped German the bird and returned a blast of his horn while Blondie next to him flashed *Moet* her breasts. German and Antonio waved and laughed as they passed them by.

The dockmaster had previously told German that the mega yacht dock couldn't accommodate them due to repairs, but when *Moet* approached, a shiny silver-gray Pershing One Forty had their spot. When German saw that, he stuffed a wad of tobacco into his mouth to smooth out his frustration. Then he spat it out over the side and walked away from the helm. A modern wide-body yacht with sleek, sexy lines had their parking place. *Moet*'s crew knew it had tremendous horsepower and was capable of traveling at cruise speeds more than thirty-eight knots. They figured it belonged to a celebrity. Still, it made German look bad.

They selected a secure mooring position with the other vessels. Antonio lowered the tender and drove it around the harbor. There were no bounces or bumps. A boardwalk made of concrete ran along the beach and the street entrance to the yacht club, a public place where local people met to eat and dance and get a release from life's hassles. That year, in the aftermath of Hurricanes Maria and Irma, the people bonded and shared a oneness that didn't require words. They rebuilt their lives. Most had lost jobs and homes, and others had lost lives, and when they stood and watched *Moet* and the Pershing, it gave them a thrill. Puerto Rican men dreamed of going to work as a crew member on one of the vessels and experiencing the adventure. Little did they know that although the jobs paid well, it got old. The help-wanted ads ran something like this:

> Large luxury yacht in need of a strong, healthy mate. Male or female. Twenty-four hours a day, seven days a week. Multitasking person required. Expert at polishing. Expert at line handling. Expert at waiting and thinking. Must have a perfect job history and no criminal record. Free room and board and computer time. Smoking and some drinking ok.

Among the people in Ponce, as in other countries, a disparity ran in the discussion of politics between husbands and wives, families and friends. While the United States had sent aid to help the recovery, politicians had big pockets to fill. Alternatively, the people found happiness in their music, their camaraderie, and their hopes that life would one day be good again, feelings never realized by Mariana. Hulia understood loss all too well.

At dinnertime, Antonio and Tomas put the ladies in the tender and took Mariana and Hulia over to the yacht club. While Mariana and Hulia dined, the men strolled over to the locals' area to wait for them. Antonio and Tomas walked beyond the yacht club property, where the wealthy yacht club members were cheering on yard games with their children and cooking on grills. Beyond the guardhouse to the club, people of minimal means climbed the stairs to the top of a four-story tower for a view of the harbor. Teenagers went up there on their own away from their mom and dad to sneak a smooch or cop a feel with their sweetheart. From there, they looked and saw hordes of large snook frantically feeding on top of each other in the water. On the dock below, little boys had their fishing poles in, but the fish were too smart to be caught on a hook. The boys screamed and grumbled when they brought in their lines and found their bait stolen without even a tug.

Stretched out along the water, there were open-air restaurants and bars and small concessions of face painters, hair braiders, and shops selling T-shirts, hats, and flip-flops. Little children and stray dogs took over a fountain to cool off from the heat. They squealed as the water sprang up at them intermittently. The very young ones danced and played naked while Grandma watched after them.

Antonio sat down at one of the bars and ordered a beer. He and Tomas grabbed the last two stools, and two well-rounded dark-haired cuties began smiling and talking to them in English. Tomas liked that. He joked with them without hesitation or asking Antonio for support. For a change, he translated for Antonio. Just as the conversation became interesting, to the dismay of the two women, Antonio got a text from Mariana. She and Hulia were finished.

"No, no, stay here and party with us," one woman said to Tomas.

"We have to go," Antonio admonished in Spanish. "We have a boss." And he pointed to *Moet* out there in the harbor. Both girls giggled.

"Take us with you."

Tomas held up his hands and smiled at them as they got off their stools and backed away.

Mariana and Hulia were bored with the yacht club restaurant. The food was good, but it was only Mariana and Hulia, the bartender, and one waiter. The two hot-blooded Latin women all dressed up in Versace and Coco Chanel needed an audience, and there was not one there. They should have tagged along with Tomas and Antonio. Through the windows of the yacht club, they could see into the Pershing at the dock. An outstanding example of modern shipbuilding. The owner of the Pershing sat over there, smoking and drinking alone. When he saw them from his boat, he sent an invitation through the bartender for them to come for a tour and a drink. "Maybe tomorrow," Mariana replied. "*Gracias.*"

As they waited in the lounge for Antonio and Tomas, Mariana shuffled through advertisements on a table. A magazine listed the best new downtown restaurants, shops, and historical places to visit. She stuffed the magazine in her bag along with *Cruising News of the Caribbean*. They would make decisions on the following day's plans over a drink on *Moet*.

Ponce, a large city, had plenty available to the ladies and the crew. Downtown Ponce had more to offer—a metropolitan area with lots of history, dining, and shopping. Antonio knew of a marine store for water filters and backup parts for the port engine and a new security alarm system. Tomas wanted to take the tender for a ride close to the coast, and German wanted to gamble at the nearby hotel and casino on his off time. He could get a woman there.

When they returned aboard after dinner, they sat reading the options for lunch the next day. There were so many good restaurants, including one that had a fashion show in a boutique-style hotel. Ending up their day, they wanted to visit the Don Q. Seralles Castle, which sat on top of a small mountain above the city. It held the distinction of housing the largest family-owned business in all of Puerto Rico, Don Q. Rum.

In the *Caribbean News*, there were articles about Saint Thomas and Sint Maarten and the progress of rebuilding. They read about the drawbridge entering Sint Maarten's harbor and the condition of the docks. Under the area titled "Recent News," Hulia read a short article about a missing boat. And beneath it was a photo of its crew. It was Tomas. He had his arm around a cute petite woman with freckles and short wispy hair. She held the fluffy white Chandon in her arms. The caption beneath reading, "Tom and Meg Trumbo and their dog, Bitti. Their boat, a sixty-one foot Viking sport fisher *Tori's Seacret*." Hulia sat motionless on the lounger while Tom poured a glass of port over her shoulder and put a plate of Stilton cheese on the table between her and Mariana. When he left, she rolled up the newsletter and slapped Mariana on the arm with it.

"You need to see this, girlfriend."

Day one's visit to Ponce began with that. First thing, German made arrangements for a private car to take them to lunch, shopping, and the Seralles Castle. At lunch and after a glass of Pinot, Mariana tearfully confessed to Hulia.

"I have Chandon's collar in my bedside table. Her name is Bitti, not Chandon. I intended to toss it over the rail but found it the next morning on the deck. That's all I know about them," she swore to Hulia as she made a sign of the cross on her chest. Then she told the whole story about how they'd found him and the dog in the water as they traveled from Cancun to Luperón. He had no memory of any details, just knew that they'd found him. Hulia listened attentively like she would want Mariana to do. Like all besties do at lunch over a glass of wine or two. Things were always said in confidence, like in the confessional. How many Hail Marys would Mariana have to say to repent for that? They laughed.

"What were you thinking, Mar? Did you think you could keep them both on board like pets forever?" Hulia pointed her stretched index finger at Mariana.

"I think you need to contact Hymie and tell him your story."

"Hulie, why? We saved their lives."

"When this Tomas finds out, he could come after you for who knows what."

After their check came and Mariana stopped crying, they fixed their eyes and lips in the room marked *Damas* and headed down the street for shopping. Before long, Hulia and Mariana were oohing and aahing in a store specializing in silk fabrics and styles. There were shoes to die for with heels so high that only a *chica* could wear them. All the while, Mariana thought of her moments with Tomas. She did not feel guilty at all; she was feeling fearful of the repercussions. Could this be kidnapping? And her crew could be witness to the facts. Her daughter and her lawyer, Hymie, would be irritated with her again, and Max would use it against her. Mariana courted trouble regularly. Hymie worked endlessly to keep her in line. He told her, "Mariana, if you break the rules, you will find trouble. Life can throw enough at you on its own. Don't look for it."

"Oh, Hymie." She would smile like a child. "I don't mean to; it finds me."

The Seralles Museum, built by the son of the original Seralles rum maker and exporter, was now a tourist spot. The museum was ultimately owned by the Ponce municipality and received funding from the government for upkeep. Beyond tours, they hosted weddings and other social events. The grounds of the museum were colored with red-orange bougainvillea trees. The building had once been the family home; the stucco walls remained painted white with an orange barrel tile roof and black wrought iron railings. They enclosed the balconies and the winding steps to the top level. It was a beautifully maintained piece of history in every way imaginable; the view of the city and the harbor beyond were beautiful too.

When Mariana and Hulia had completed the tour, it was time to sit and relax. They sat on a bench near the dinghy dock waiting for Antonio. This allowed the owner of the silver-gray Pershing to dash out on his gang-plank in his silk smoking jacket. He resembled the sleuth Sherlock, with his cigarette holder hanging out the side of his mouth. He pursed his lips to hold it in place and then removed it as he extended an invitation for the two of them to come for cocktails. He caught Mariana off guard. Lack of excuses by Mariana and encouragement by Hulia set the evening in motion, six thirty that night.

After boarding *Moet*, Mariana expressed her feelings to Hulia.

"Hulie, I really didn't want to accept his invitation, but I will go because you want to."

Mariana told Tomas their plans and cautioned him about dinnertime.

"Sometimes, these things go on way too late. Maybe we could set it up that if we don't return by eight thirty, you can call with an excuse—let's say a concern with Chandon."

Tomas got it and gave her a nod, and at six thirty, Antonio took them to the dock where the Pershing sat tied. Once aboard, Rory, the owner, took them for a tour of the yacht. It was not larger than *Moet*, but it was new and decorated Scandinavian contemporary. In comparison, *Moet*'s design was traditional. Hulia and Mariana were both in awe of the décor, and it made

Mariana think she wanted a new boat. The high points of five staterooms and heads—and the factory-equipped galley with up-to-date appliances—impressed her. It also slept five crew members. Rory introduced himself to them again. Yachts were his business. He was an executive with the Ferretti Group, the manufacturer of his Pershing. Pershing planned to preview a new 170 footer in Monaco. It was all he could talk about.

"You girls should come to Europe and see the new model."

"Yeah, right, we'll just hop on over," Mariana whispered under her breath in Hulia's ear. Hulia turned and gave her a look.

Mariana became bored with all the talk of corporate politics, while Hulia seemed taken in by it all. Rory's monotone voice matched his facial expression like it would crack if he smiled. The man came across full of himself. The girls knew the type, but he might be a convenient man to know.

Rory bragged about being fluent in Spanish as well as Chinese and French. But since neither she nor Hulia spoke Chinese or French, Rory could have said "shit" to them in those languages, and they wouldn't have known the difference. He looked their age. Mariana figured that Rory desired companionship for the evening. Of course, Rory didn't tell them that, but Mariana could tell, and Hulia could too. He anxiously shared the photography work he did while traveling in Africa, and Hulia let him. His photos were quite good, and when the call came from Tomas, at eight thirty, Hulia said to Mariana, "I am really enjoying seeing all this; do you mind if I stay a little longer? I am sure Rory can arrange for a ride for me later."

"Forgive me, Rory, but I am exhausted after today's sightseeing, and I hate to disappoint my chef when he made us such a wonderful dinner. Hulia, I will have Tomas put a portion aside for you." Although both girls knew Hulia probably wouldn't return that night. Hulia agreed, and Mariana apologized one more time as she climbed on the tender when Antonio arrived. Not an unusual routine for their relationship; when they were much younger, they'd used one another to meet or lose men.

For that night's meal, Tomas prepared a chicken cutlet breaded with panko in a white butter wine sauce. And he got ready to make a second for Hulia. He smiled at Mariana from the galley when she returned. Angeli washed and pressed his chef's jacket and checkered pants. Mariana looked down at his feet and saw a pair of white clogs.

"We probably won't see Hulia tonight, Tomas, and if we do, she probably won't want dinner."

He brought her plate to the table. The butter made it golden brown, and he added grilled asparagus on the side of the plate. He put couscous on a smaller plate on her left. Mariana didn't eat much, and after, she sat alone on the deck, watching the Pershing and thinking about her situation. Tomas stayed with her for a while, and anyone seeing them would view their relationship as platonic, but as the evening continued, they moved up to the flybridge, where Mariana had spent many a night with Max naked under the stars. This time with Tomas. She gave him all he wanted from her, and then she sent him away to his cabin. Mariana was her name, and drama was her game, and it haunted her. She required love and attention. She'd grown up with parents she rarely saw and had been raised alone by wealthy grandparents. She spent her life searching for romance, but when she found it, things always went south for her.

Before she turned in, she called German; they needed to talk in the morning about where next and when. After that, and before he said good night, German told her some bad news. She closed her eyes and held her breath because she already knew. The most recent word from the dockmaster was that a missing couple off a boat had been sighted. The man had been sighted in the Dominican Republic, his wife in Cuba with the boat.

German set Mariana in a stew. She lay in her bed, thinking, trying to figure out how to indemnify her actions. What were her choices? Maybe she should talk to Tomas first thing in the morning. After all, she had saved his life, and except for the dog's name, she hadn't lied to him.

I only just yesterday saw the newsletter at the yacht club, she said to herself.

Sleep needed to happen for Mariana. She opened her bottle of purple hearts and took three.

Early the next morning, against Hulia's recommendation, Mariana went into the galley to find Tomas. She walked up behind him and turned in front of him; she stroked his hair around his ears and kissed him. Mariana took the Hublot watch she'd purchased for him in Punta Cana from her robe pocket. She had wrapped it in the marina newsletter, a mistake set in motion.

"When we were in Punta Cana shopping, I saw this most incredible timepiece. I felt bad that you had nothing of your own when we found you, except for the dog."

When he saw it, he started with a smile of humble gratitude, but then he began to comprehend her Spanish combined with her English words.

What did she mean, except for the dog? Tomas's lazy eyebrows drew tight at the bridge of his nose. What was she talking about? Then she cried, and it confused him.

Tomas eyed the newsletter and saw the picture of Meg and the dog and then him. A lot for Tom's fragile mind to process. But he could read English. His mind watched a video running backward, and he couldn't put it on hold. Out of her other pocket, Mariana pulled Bitti's collar, with her name engraved on it. The newsletter had the number of the US Coast Guard in Key West, and it noted, "For further information."

Mariana saw anger run all over Tomas. He jerked away from her and clenched his teeth. He wiped his hands on his pants to get her stink off him. He wanted no part of her. Tomas saw himself as a fool for the pleasure of this woman. Not done with her yet, he grabbed her shoulders and shook her. Then he released her in shame. Mariana cowered away from him.

"No," Mariana managed to squeak out. "We have news, good news, please." And Tomas stepped away from her.

"There is news that she is in Havana with the boat and safe."

Just as this altercation occurred, German strolled into the galley. Tomas looked at German and then at Mariana.

"Then you will take me there; tell your captain." Tomas walked out past him, and German's lips spat a ball of foam at Mariana.

"I told you this day would come. You know this means trouble for us."

"What do you mean, 'Us'? I am responsible, not you. I will pay any price that needs to be paid."

"I pay the price if he sues you or you are prosecuted for kidnapping. I hope I have a job after all this."

"My God man, we saved his life," Mariana countered.

100

"I have always been here for you, Mariana, and I have seen what's been going on here."

"Don't talk to me this way, German. I will do as I please."

Mariana's head began to swirl. Yes, German put her husband and his bitch off *Moet*. Mariana remembered the night they'd lie before her in her cabin, bodies entwined. In her cabin. The only remedy for Max's betrayal of her was as German told her. He'd left them for dead afloat in a life raft. So he told her.

Mariana often had blackouts when she drank, especially when combined with the purple hearts. Max and German had both taken advantage of that. At Max's request, after the incident in the cabin, it was German who had arranged for Max and Camilla's private transport to shore after she found them in her bed, and it was Mariana that German had betrayed. He didn't really put them adrift. He radioed shore and they were picked up quickly. But he didn't want Mariana to know that. German would never sever his relationship with Max. Max took that episode as an opportunity to leave Mariana and set up her drinking and drugging as grounds for divorce and get a piece of her fortune as his alimony.

CHAPTER NINE
A Smiley Pup

In Havana, Meg began to prepare to go home. She called Patrick, a boat captain for hire. He could fly in and take *Tori's Seacret* to the Florida Keys. He had done work captaining for them in the past and was a man to be trusted. Meg would fly home to Miami. The news that she was alive had filtered to friends. Meg received emails and phone calls happy that she'd survived but sad that there was no news about Tom. She didn't dwell on it. She kept busy. The sooner she got home, the sooner she could get help to find Tom.

She went to the dockmaster and discussed her plans. When Patrick could get her an arrival day, she could buy her airline ticket.

The dockmaster asked her, "Is your husband taking the boat?"

"No," she said. Then she discussed her situation with him. The dockmaster already knew from the talk on the dock.

"Do you have documents that prove you are the owner?"

Meg became silent. She had never considered it a problem. Tom's trust held it. Even though she remained the beneficiary, in Cuba, they might impound it if she attempted to take it without documents. The dockmaster treated her kindly, but he had to comply with the law.

People were walking in and out of the office, and his phone wouldn't stop. He suggested she take a seat in the lobby, and as soon as he could, he would make a few calls to see the best way to handle her problem. She didn't want to go home and leave the boat behind, but she realized she may not have a choice.

She sat and waited. She could call Ann and Silvio to ask for guidance. But asking them would only be a last resort. They had their hands full with Jhosep. Two scruffy men with Santa Claus beards opened the screen door to the marina office and moseyed past her. They peeked into the dockmaster's office, and the dockmaster motioned for them to sit outside in the waiting area. There were only two seats available, and they were next to Meg.

They've been at sea a few months, phew, Meg thought as a text came in on her phone. Her screen saver lit up. Aw, a picture of her Bitti.

"What a cute dog," one man said. "Traveling with you?"

"No, not now," she sadly responded.

"Just saw a dog like that in Luperón, where we were anchored."

"Yes, there are a lot of little white dogs like her," she said, trying to pay attention to what was going on in the dockmaster's office.

"She sure is white and clean. That dog was very clean. And that dog smiled. The darnedest thing."

Meg smiled, trying again to be polite.

"And the guy walking her, all red like from hell, all burned up from the sun or something."

Again she smiled at them as the dockmaster waved her into his office with the news. The news was no news. He suggested she go to the boat and wait until he knew more.

"Be patient; things move slowly here at this time of the day. People are at lunch. As soon as I know, I'll come to your boat." And he smiled as he talked with another customer and shuffled her out the door. With all the activity there, it might be a while.

At the boat, she gave Patrick a call with an update of the situation and suggested he wait until she heard more. As the day's end drew near, she brought out a bottle of wine, took a glass and a cooler, and sat out on the boat to pass the time. Meg watched boats of all sizes and makes coming and going. Charter fishing boats going out for big game fish and privately owned vessels like hers coming in for dockage.

A few short weeks ago, Meg's life had changed. Maybe she would just get a flight home, leave the boat, get the documents, and return. She needed her daughter or a close friend to give her guidance. But could she return? She started realizing the boat meant nothing to her without Tom. She needed to forget about the boat. She made up her mind: tomorrow she'd go home.

The two guys she'd met in the marina office walked along the dock with water and a case of beer. They were docked ten slips from *Tori's Seacret*. They stopped to talk.

"You have an awesome boat. You have a partner?"

"No." Meg hesitated. "I am alone." Should she have said that? "My husband is coming."

One said, "Hey, come and eat with us. My brother is frying fish tonight, and he's a wonderful cook. We have plenty." Meg didn't want to get involved.

"Thank you, but no, I have things to do here."

"You seem lonely, and we don't bite. We are just hoping for some conversation in plain English. Come on." They pleaded with her.

They're harmless, Meg thought. "Ok, but only if I can bring some wine; you guys drink wine?" Meg found herself teasing with them.

"Yeah!" They drew the *yeah* out in harmony. "We have been talking to ourselves for more than a month."

"I'll come in about forty minutes, but I won't stay late."

The dockmaster's office would be closed by that time, and if she hadn't heard from him by then, she wouldn't get any news until morning. At six o'clock, Meg grabbed two bottles of white and went to their sloop. Although they liked their beer, she should have brought four. They were Billy and Bob. Billy had red frizzy hair, and Bob had none. They sat and talked at a picnic table that one of the guys had covered with a Mickey Mouse beach towel as a substitute tablecloth. He set the table with turquoise Melmac plates from the sixties. They were scratched, but they were scrubbed clean. They each had a beer from a bottle and then moved on to the wine in glasses that Meg had brought with her. First, they talked about Paducah, Kentucky, where they'd lived all of their lives. Two brothers, one divorced, one widowed. They talked about how all of their lives they'd sailed the lakes near their home and into the Lake of the Ozarks. The waves on those big lakes could get pretty treacherous in a storm. Totally different from navigating the Caribbean, but it gave them experience.

Meg talked about the time years ago when she'd driven through Paducah during an ice storm and the roads and town had been shut down for days, the ice crystals so thick on the electrical wires that they hung too low to the ground for cars to drive under them, and the trees snapped from the weight of the ice. She'd gotten one of the last rooms at an Econo Lodge that took the big dog that traveled with her. They remembered that storm.

The two brothers talked about how they sailed down the Mississippi and into the Gulf of Mexico. They hugged the coast of Florida and stopped here and there to take on water and dump their trash.

"We've found that a lot of the marinas along the coast of Florida weren't thrilled to give a slip to a sloop like ours. We don't spend much money and usually only spend a night or two. They call us WAFIs." He laughed.

"What are WAFIs?" Meg laughed.

"Excuse my French. Wind-assisted fuckin' idiots."

"You know," Billy said, "when people see a couple of guys like us on a sailboat alone, they figure we're gay. But for Bob and me, we've been boating all of our lives. And now that we both are alone, we figured what the heck; we'd do that bucket list from the movie."

Meg asked, "So, where you been?"

"We been to the Bahamas a few times, each time visiting islands we had never been to before. People don't realize that there are over seven hundred islands in the Bahamas, even though only thirty of them are inhabited. When someone says they are going to the Bahamas, everyone thinks Nassau or Grand Bahama. But these other islands are remote, and the more remote it gets, the better it gets. The fish and conch and lobster become bigger and more plentiful. It's all for the taking. From there, we went to South Caicos and anchored there and found thousands of little footprints from conch making paths in the sand. They made a little village. We took pictures, but it didn't do justice to their underwater world."

Meg added that she and Tom had been there also and seen it too. They all agreed they'd go back in a minute.

"Then we made the long grueling trip to Luperón in the Dominican Republic. The place we told you about that we saw the little white dog. It's a great anchorage. They had a good restaurant with a bar built into a giant kapok tree. There were several sailboats in there and, one night, one big beautiful yacht. It was lit up from pulpit to the stern."

Then she asked, "So why didn't you continue on, since you came so far?"

The one brother confessed, "I am not well; I need to get to the States, where I can see a doctor and take advantage of my Medicare."

Meg agreed in her mind that he hadn't appeared healthy when she first met them in the office. He seemed unusually thin, and the whites of his eyes were yellow, and his skin was a green gray. The brother who fried the fish did an excellent job, just like his brother said. He used a small portable fryer on the dock. He scooped the fish out of the bubbling oil when the breading turned a golden brown. When he cut it, the fish flaked apart on the serving platter. Tom always said there was nothing like white and tender fresh fried fish. Bob put out a cabbage slaw mixed with chunky blue cheese dressing, bacon bits, and onion. A unique combination that went well with the fish and a perfect alternative to a green salad.

After dinner, they sat out on the dock, and Bob got out his banjo and strummed a few country and western oldies. Billy sang Roy Roger's "Cowboy Night Herd" tune. And when he started to yodel, others crowded close to the table. Billy and Bob were two decent guys. She didn't know if, in fact, they indeed were brothers, and she didn't care; they were just nice guys. She was glad that she'd gone.

That day had been busy, which could mean a good night's sleep for Meg. She went and had one more glass of wine, got into bed, and fell asleep. Lying on her back, she suddenly found herself staring wide eyed at the ceiling of her cabin when it hit her. Could the little dog that the brothers spoke about have been Bitti? And the sunburned man, her Tom? The time frame could have been right. She could hardly wait until dawn to go back to the brothers' boat for more information. She got up and got the coffee brewing and sat huddled in the salon, thinking. When the darkness gave way, and she could see, she ran to their sailboat slip. She could only see the light at the tip of their mast as it passed through the inlet out to sea.

Meg let out a coyote howl. She shocked herself and looked around to see if anyone heard her. Meg cursed herself for not listening, not asking more questions, not putting two and two together—for not going to their boat during the night when she woke up. She knew then that she had to get to that small anchorage in the Dominican Republic. Meg knew in her heart that Tom survived, but now her head knew it too. Pieces of a puzzle were waiting for Meg in Luperón. She had to go there.

Meg excitedly called her daughter, Carol—woke her up and told her the news. Carol wanted to believe that this could all be true. That her father could be found alive someplace in the Caribbean and that her mother would find him. But she tried to dissuade her mother from traveling there and told her again to come home. But Carol knew her mother, and whether by air or by sea, her mom would get to Luperón.

It would have been a very long way for her to take *Tori's Seacret* from Havana to Luperón. Plus, the Cuban government wouldn't allow her to leave with the boat. She considered getting a person from home to fly to the Dominican Republic and go to Luperón, but no one would follow up like she would. He was her man. And she had to go.

She and Tom had been in Luperón once, ten years previous, and she knew of the bay that the brothers spoke about. She remembered the sparsely populated town, but that's all she remembered. They had visited many anchorages and it had been a long time ago.

There were flights from Havana to Puerto Plata in the Dominican Republic regularly, and then it was a few hours' drive west to Luperón. Meg made her reservations with the help of the dockmaster and called Ann and Silvio at home.

"Ann, this is Meg Trumbo. I have wonderful news. I have news about my husband's whereabouts." Meg didn't explain how she'd come to find it. "I am leaving later on today. I feel terrible leaving so soon after Jhosep's stroke, but I need to go now."

"No, Meg, we understand. He is doing well, much better today. There doesn't seem to be any permanent damage. Thankfully, you acted fast and got him to the hospital."

"That is so good to hear, Ann. My flight leaves at one thirty. Maybe I can get by the hospital to say goodbye on my way."

"He would like that, I am sure. I will come and get you, and we can stop by the hospital on the way to the airport. What about your boat, can we help you with it in any way?"

"The dockmaster here recommended a man, but I am worried just leaving it with someone I don't know. It could become a problem."

"I agree with you. I will call Silvio at his office. He knows a lot of people who know a lot of people. Jhosep may know someone too."

They agreed on a time when Ann would pick her up. Meg knew that when she told Ann and Silvio about how she'd gotten her information, they would be skeptical. They'd expect that she'd return soon when she found out her trip to Luperón brought nothing.

Meg brought in all the cushions, covered the teak cockpit table and the chairs. She went up in the flybridge and covered the helm seats, and closed the access panel to the electronics. Then she turned off the engine switches and hid a key to the boat in one of the fish boxes in the cockpit floor like Tom always did. When she opened it, she drew back in distress. Meg looked down at the tiny yellow vireo in the water that puddled in the box. It lay on its' side taking in shallow breaths. Meg thought it had flown away, but it must have hidden and gotten washed there the day she cleaned the boat. Meg went back inside the boat and grabbed an old towel, two pieces of bread, and a small plastic bowl with water. She added it all to a shoebox, cut holes in the lid for air, and then carefully lay the hitchhiker inside.

Out in front of the marina with a few articles of clothing and personal items in her backpack, Meg stood at the spot where Jhosep had picked her up the day before. What a horrible day that had been. Especially for him. When the car pulled up, in the driver's seat, she saw Silvio alone without Ann.

Meg did like Silvio. She'd put those feelings in their place where they belonged the other night, and Meg was satisfied. She jumped in the car, and together they sped away to the hospital.

"Ann said she would come for me," Meg said. Then she sat quietly.

"If you give me a day, I can arrange to go with you on this goose hunt."

Meg wanted to laugh. "You mean, 'Wild goose chase.' Seriously, Silvio. That's very kind of you, but I need to go alone."

"You will probably be returning tomorrow, you know."

"Ok, then, if that is the case, I will see you all then."

Silvio waited in the car. Meg ran in to say goodbye to Jhosep. She caught him on a gurney outside his room. The technician taking him to radiology for more testing stopped and stepped aside so they could talk. Meg told Jhosep her news. He didn't react negatively. He understood she had to go. He had rescued her, and she'd returned the favor at the café on the street. They said their goodbyes. When Jhosep heard that Silvio was waiting for her at the curb, his heavy brows frowned at her, and he pointed his finger at her.

"I love my son. But you be careful, Meg. He is a hound." Meg knew, and the blush on her showed she agreed.

Meg and Silvio's relationship ended before it had begun. On the way to the airport, not many words were spoken between them. Meg would find Tom, and when she did, they'd pick up their life where it left off. She would never cross the line. She knew it, and Silvio knew it too. Before Meg got out of the car, she took the shoebox and handed it to Silvio.

"This is for Juan. Tell him to take care of this little survivor for me."

It took two hours to fly to Puerto Plata. When she arrived there, she tried to hire a taxi to take her to Luperón, but she found no takers. The distance, the mountain roads, and the time of day created a problem. She chose to get a room in Puerto Plata and go to Luperón the next morning.

The roosters crowed, announcing the dawn. Meg rented a scooter and a helmet from the Scooter Doctor next door to her motel. She had ridden one once before. Meg wore a baseball hat under the German military helmet to protect herself from lice. They gave her a map, and she noted landmarks and circled intersections to find her way. With the scooter, if Meg needed to stay longer, she could. Meg called her daughter to let her know she had arrived in Puerto Plata and was on her way to Luperón—but Meg didn't tell her how.

The rainy season of Puerto Plata produced a cloudy, clammy morning for Meg. The ride took Meg from roughly paved city streets to winding roads, up and down hills that graduated into mountains. There were no road signs that she could see, only minor landmarks like a rock or a dilapidated shack where you would turn left, then right. Along with the altitude, sharp curves increased. Crucifixes with plastic flowers affixed to them were planted next to the road. Beneath them lay the bodies of loved ones that careened off the cliff. What a sad legacy that would be for Meg. She decreased her speed.

Meg passed women with baskets of vegetables on their heads, pulling sheep on rope leashes. Dirty children with runny noses tagged behind. She stopped at a roadside stand and got a lunch specialty, like a taco, the meat questionable but tasty. It may have been goat. A small bottle of Coca-Cola washed it down. Not cold, but safe to drink. She pointed at the intersecting road and asked the man at the stand, "Luperón?"

He said, "*Sí.*"

Meg said, "*Gracias.*"

Her watch said 2:00 p.m. when she arrived in Luperón, and she went to the only place she knew to go, the bar perched high above the anchorage that the brothers had talked about. The same bar that she and Tom had visited ten years ago. Empty at that time of the day except for the bartender. In the distance, she could see the mountains of Haiti. Overcast there also, and rain clouds hung low. Meg could also see the beach where the brothers said they saw Bitti and the man and the fancy lady. She parked and dismounted her scooter, pulled the helmet off her head while trying to fluff up her hair. Meg found a restroom shared by the staff and the patrons, where they stacked five-gallon buckets of peanut oil. One look in the mirror, she took a piece of paper towel and wiped the road dirt off her face.

The bartender, a rather young fellow, spoke English. She asked about a boat at anchorage within the last few weeks, a man with a bad sunburn, and a dog, a little white dog. He said there might have been, yes. "But a lot of boats come and go."

"Did you see their boat?"

"I remember a lady and a white dog, and three men in the restaurant. A yacht in Bahia Blanco for the night. She may have been on it, the fancy lady. I do remember because the men took turns dancing with her." The name of the yacht, no, he didn't see or know the name.

"It is a distance, you see," he said as he pointed. "If you go to the dock in the town of Luperón, the commandant there will have records with the name. If you give him a tip, he will probably find it for you. He's required to keep records."

He told her how to go to get to the town dock. She gave him a five-dollar bill, probably more than she needed to, and headed off on her scooter onto the road winding down to the water.

Two men sat at a square table and played dominoes on the porch outside the commandant's office. Meg motioned to one and then to the desk inside. He smiled at her and shook his head no and moved a tile. Meg waited awhile and then walked to a pharmacy to buy a bottle of water and sat in the shade on a bench. Meg continued to wait, watching the two men and thinking she might be taken for a fool. Not much action there except for a pack of potcakes. They were inbreds that ran in the street and there were two that were humping. They paid no attention to Meg. Meg glanced over to the water in the bay, and it lacked clarity. Not what she'd expected or remembered from her previous visit. After thirty minutes and just before she stood to search for other advice, the bartender drove up in a white cargo van, and all three men entered the office. The sight of him gave her relief, and she walked over. The time was getting late, and the ride to Puerto Plata in the dark was not part of her plan. Of course, not much these days went as planned.

One of the men at the game table sat at the desk in the office. He resembled an older version of the bartender. The bartender started speaking to him in Spanish and then to Meg.

"My father is the commandant. What is your name, senora?"

"My name is Meg Trumbo."

He repeated her name to his father and introduced her. He began saying more; she assumed repeating the questions she'd asked him at the bar. His father opened a drawer and pulled out an accordion file folder with numbers on its pockets that represented the numerical days of the month. For some of the days in the folder, he pulled out five boat papers, and for some days he pulled only one boat clearing in or out. Then he pulled paperwork out on one boat and smiled big as he shared it with her. The son smiled at Meg too. Then the third man smiled also. It had come in from Cancun, Mexico. Next port, Punta Cana in the Dominican Republic. It was dated July 3. The yacht's name: *Moet*. Meg read the paperwork, made a note of the boat's name—and its captain's name, German Veneto. She wrote his name on her map. The manifest listed the passengers and the crew members by name. No Tom Trumbo aboard.

"I told you if you give him a tip, he would probably help."

Meg tried to smile when she forked over another five. She asked about a hotel, and he said yes, one, nearby. Casa del Sol, House of the Rising Sun. The name made her think of the song. Another favorite of theirs. Could that be a sign?

Meg pushed her bike up the street a few blocks, weaving around holes and rocks as he'd directed and found the inn. A yellow-gold house built of concrete with red barrel roof tiles. Star jasmine bushes covered a concrete fence. The fragrance was familiar to her. Over a gated archway, a rookie had hand-painted a vine of red roses. Under that, a yellow sun carved from a piece of wood displayed the name of the inn, Casa del Sol. An older lady came out to the front porch with a broom and greeted her. Round faced, with shiny black hair, she wore a white dress with a red apron tied on her plump belly. She had a cell phone in her pocket and a Bluetooth in her ear. Not a likely sight, but communication was everywhere except when Meg needed it.

"Oh, I see my grandson sent you to me." Again, Meg smiled and grimaced because she was running out of fives. The family had converted their home to an inn. The living room and dining room were filled with heavy, dark ornamental furniture. Tchotchkes crowded every inch of every tabletop, shelf, and counter. When Meg's eyes took it in, she whispered to herself, "Lord, don't let this be me."

The inn offered bed and breakfast and supper in the evening. Meg appreciated it after her day and the day that lay before her. A rejuvenated spirit was within Meg's body. She'd gotten what she came for, and Meg knew where to go next. She sensed the scent of her man like a snake on a hunt for prey. Now she had crumbs to follow. Meg didn't know about the fancy lady aboard the yacht *Moet*, but she knew her Tom loved her.

Nan Prodan

CHAPTER TEN

Deception

The following morning Meg woke up to the sound of another boisterous rooster outside her bedroom window. He stood on a decaying pile of debris, jumped off, and strutted as he showed off to his hens.

"Come on, come on. Get up," she swore it said. "It's raining."

Meg jumped up; it was still dark, and yes, the rain poured straight down. The clouds she saw hanging over the mountains of Haiti moved over Casa del Sol in Luperón. Meg had that scooter ride to Puerto Plata in the rain. She got herself together and dressed in the same dirty clothing as the day before. Meg went out to the lobby area. Next to it in the dining room, Meg found orange juice, scrambled eggs, bacon, toast, and a fresh pot of coffee on the table. More than she needed. Jesus and his mother, Margo, came in from the kitchen.

"Did you sleep well?" Margo asked in chopped-up English.

"Yes, very comfortable bed. I needed a good night's rest." And then Meg turned to Jesus. "I want to thank you for your help and hospitality; as soon as the rain lets up a little, I am going to be leaving for Puerto Plata." She got out her wallet and looked to Margo. "Can I settle my bill now?"

Jesus took her money for the room and handed it to his mother, who then stormed from the room. "I can take you and haul your scooter in my van. I need to go anyway, for inventory for the bar."

"Oh my gosh, thank you so much; I couldn't imagine the trip in the rain and the mud," Meg said in relief while taking in Margo's reaction.

Jesus looked sad, half apologizing for the scene. "She doesn't remember. She thinks I am her grandson. It is a sad time of life for her."

Meg felt terrible. She understood. Meg wished to could go and find her and console her, like she had done with her own mother, but it would serve no purpose except for Meg.

Jesus's offer came as a blessing for Meg. Meg had found out the day before that her scootering days were over. Jesus loaded the bike in his van and rolled down the windows, and they left for Puerto Plata. To keep dry from the rain coming in, Meg slid over closer to the middle of the bench seat next to Jesus. His words competed with the road noise, and she dipped in to hear him speak. Talking helped pass the time. The slippery road and Jesus's speed going into the curves made the ride nerve racking. Meg rocked and bounced in her seat, and she grabbed hold of the dashboard to stabilize herself. Twice an animal ran out in front of them, and Jesus had to swerve left, then right and left again, to avoid running into a ravine. When she looked down there, she saw an overturned shell of a car. Jesus just smiled at her and continued on like it was all another day. The veins in Meg's neck stood out, and her jaw tightened simultaneously. She struggled to hide her fear. Meg was a grateful passenger on Jesus's rodeo ride.

When the mountains turned to hills again, the bumpy road became a paved road filled with cars and trucks and scooters. They passed one man driving a scooter with a woman behind him on the seat. She held her baby on her knee, while her tiny legs dangled freely while she slept. Only the man wore a helmet. They were heading into Puerto Plata for the day's business. A group of wild dogs ran alongside them, just below her window. She thought surely that Jesus would hit the leader that darted in and out in front of the van and the other dogs. She let out a squeal, and Jesus tilted his head and explained.

"The leader would rather die than give up his spot in the pack. That's the way here."

At the rental company, Jesus got the bike out of the truck and waited. In no time at all, she made the return, and they continued on to the bus terminal a mile off the main highway. Meg searched in her wallet for money to pay him, but Jesus said no.

"Mi madre and padre say to help you. You are a good person, and we are good people. Remember my people that way. Maybe we will meet again, and you can repay me."

"*Gracias*, thank you."

When she exited the van, he leaned over and said, "I hope you find your dog and your husband. He's a lucky guy."

"Thank you, me too," Meg called out to him as she opened her umbrella, but he pulled out and was on his way before she could get it out of her mouth.

There were two tourist buses lined up waiting for travelers, one headed south to Santa Domingo, the capital, the other east to Punta Cana. Meg went to the window, bought her ticket, and climbed aboard. A five-hour trip, not leaving for another two hours. She bunched up her backpack on the window and lay her head against it and closed her eyes. When she did, she could see Tom, the last night in Key West, and the day of the wave. How he took control and the fear in his eyes. Meg heard a crash. Meg opened her eyes to see a group of tourists entering the bus, all keyed up, throwing their gear on the bus. In spite of all the noise, she dozed off again, wondering if her search would end in Punta Cana at the marina.

A massive man in a sweaty green uniform climbed on and hollered out and waved a ticket in the air. He set a cage that held an enormous ruffled, feathered rooster next to the driver's seat. He resembled the bird with his wiry spiked hair and his sharp hooked nose.

The people in the Dominican Republic loved cockfighting. The men went out with their roosters to the fighting ring on Saturday night and laid their pesos down. Meg couldn't help but pity the bird.

"Punta Cana, Punta Cana," the driver called out.

He hauled himself through the aisle, bumping patrons' shoulders while he collected the tickets. He closed the door, put on loud merengue music, and pulled out of the terminal. The bumpy ride got bumpier as the afternoon passed. The rain stopped, and the sky cleared. The hot sun made it difficult for the bus's air conditioner to keep the heat and the humidity out. Meg turned, and the seats behind her were filled with passengers sound asleep or fingering their cell phones. Meg saw that she didn't fit in among the other passengers. Meg had never traveled alone like that before. She took a rag from her backpack and poured a little water on it from a bottle and wiped her neck. The road sign that they passed pointing north to Samaná told Meg that her trip's end drew near. The marina and the yacht named *Moet* could be waiting an hour up the highway.

A few miles farther, the bus pulled over to the side of the road, and the driver called out.

"*Baño.*" The driver and a few people filed off to use the bathroom in a rest area, and before long, they were on the road. The speed of the traffic picked up, and many of the vehicles on the road were limousines. From her window, Meg saw that they were filled with the well-to-dos that had flown into the new airport nearby.

At five o'clock the bus arrived in Punta Cana. The driver dropped them at the airport, where the passengers could get taxis to complete their journey. There were many to choose from. Meg got lucky. A well-dressed family of five waited in front of her at the cabstand under the sign labeled "Marina Punta Cana." They invited Meg to share the van.

"Thank you, thank you so much. I can pay my share."

But they told Meg no, they were going anyway. "Are you meeting with friends?" they asked.

"No, my husband," Meg secretly wished. "He's here on a yacht."

"We've owned a townhome in the marina for several years, and we come with family and parents in the summertime."

"Do you own a boat?" Meg asked. Boy, what a coincidence that would be.

"No, the men golf and the kids swim. It is family reunion time." Then they commented about the big yachts that docked there.

At the guardhouse at the entrance to the complex, guests needed to show their paperwork to gain entry. That could have been a problem for Meg. When the taxi pulled up to the window, the man who had offered her the ride passed his paperwork to the entry guard. The guard assumed Meg a part of their group and waved them through, and the taxi continued on to the residences and marina area. Greenery sheathed the road. Red and purple bougainvillea flowered everywhere along the pathway. It reminded her of the drive up to Silvio and Ann's home but much grander. The tall palms trunks manicured in a pineapple design added a sensation of royalty and created a wall of trees on each side of the road.

"How about we just drop you by the marina?" the man asked Meg. As the taxi drove into the marina area, Meg's eyes searched the names on the sides of the yachts, hoping to see *Moet*.

"Which one?" a young boy in the cab asked Meg.

"I don't see it, maybe just drop me here, and I can walk there where I see more boats."

Meg called out a thank-you when she got out of the van, and they pulled away. Meg hurriedly walked on the narrow brick golf cart path, when a security guard in a cart approached her.

"Excuse me, lady, do you have a marina pass?"

"No, do I need one?"

"Come with me." Meg jumped in, and they drove away.

He drove her one street over. Meg could see a marina office sign.

Meg stood in line and waited. Her shorts and her T-shirt reeked of hot, sweaty mess, and certainly she was not a woman who might be a guest on one of the yachts. Inside, the woman at the counter asked, "Can I help you?"

"My husband's name is Tom Trumbo, and he is aboard a yacht. Its name is *Moet*. I am supposed to meet up with him here."

The woman questioned the visual of the dock layout on her computer and shook her head.

"*Moet* was here, but it is gone now."

Disappointment rushed from her head to her toes. This couldn't be happening.

"Maybe they are returning for you. Maybe you should call him." Meg didn't know how to reach Tom, and the last time she had called his cell phone in Havana, it had rung in the drawer in the boat. But she had written the captain's name on her map. She pulled it out. German Veneto.

"Well, we have the captain's cell number here, but we are not allowed to give it out. They only went to the yacht club in Ponce. It's not very far. I can give the captain a call. German is his name."

Meg knew the look on her face was getting bitchy. She covered it up with a smile and thanked her, and the woman at the counter called the number they had for German. He didn't answer, so she left him a message for him to call the marina in Punta Cana.

"Please call me if you hear from them," Meg requested and gave them her cell number.

"I really need a place to stay. Is there a place at the marina I can get short term?"

The attendant at the marina desk directed her to a hotel operated by the marina that had rooms to accommodate crew members from transient yachts.

"The season is slow now, so you might find a room without a reservation."

It turned out that the crew-quarters section of the hotel had a vacancy. A room with a view of the harbor. When the marina was built, contractors installed colossal concrete jacks that looked like they came from a game of ball and jacks thrown by a giant lying down on the beach, passing the time. The concrete jetty stretched out to the open sea and marked the inlet. After sunset, the red and green lights that marked the inlet reminded her of a runway for a jet plane.

Meg got her shower and changed into her only other shorts and T-shirt in her backpack and headed to the laundry room. On the way, she stopped in the lobby at a small market center that sold sandwiches and chips and drinks. She hadn't eaten since breakfast in Luperón, and she grabbed a chicken sandwich and a can of beer.

Down a dark hallway, a dim light lit the entrance with a soft glow. The sound of the machines tumbling and flushing water set up the scene. A woman sat alone with her back to the door on a white plastic chair, scoffing up a sandwich and paging through a magazine. Meg's peripheral vision caught a glimpse of a shadow. She got up and hurried to the security phone at the rear and began to hit 911, when the heat of liquored breath touched her neck. Meg turned to protect herself. She brought up her knee and swung it into the groin of her pursuer. He bent over in pain, and Meg whisked by him, out the door of the laundry room, into the hallway and into the lobby. No one at the desk; she darted up the stairs to her second-floor room and locked the door, her backpack, her only clothing, and her dinner left behind.

Things didn't seem to be working out well for Meg since she'd arrived in Punta Cana. That night had been disturbing. It woke her up to what Silvio had said. A woman was vulnerable traveling alone. Again, she realized how much she depended on Tom.

Meg woke up later than usual for her, surprised but knowing that she must have needed the rest. In the bathroom mirror, puffy eyes looked at her, and her light-brown hair that ordinarily fell soft and wavy stood out dry and frizzy. The days after leaving home had weighed on her mind and her body, and Meg had lost weight. A concerned friend might say she needed a spa day badly, but that would have to wait.

In the lobby, the desk clerk multitasked and held the phone to his ear with his shoulder. She stood by waiting and noticed that her backpack and clothing lay on his counter. Folded neatly on top were her bra and panties.

When he hung up, he put them in a bag and gave it to Meg. "I figured you'd be wanting these."

"I came to the desk last night after a bad experience, but you weren't here."

"I'll say. I had a bad experience too. A wild woman in the laundry room kneed me in the balls after I came to tell her she had a phone call from the marina office." Meg's face became warm. She was mortified.

"I am sorry, I thought…"

"Don't worry, I dried and folded your stuff." He embarrassed her again, and Meg blushed at the thought that he had touched her underwear.

The clerk had let his black hair grow long on top, and he piled it in a wave on his forehead. He combed the sides toward the center of his head, and the hair came together in a ducktail. His nostrils flared when he spoke. He was not a local. His voice twanged when he spoke, and he should have worn a cowboy hat and a guitar. He reminded her of Elvis before he became a hit and got fat. But the clerk had a nice smile, and he meant well. Meg had only taken one course in karate, and with no practice, who knew she would have such good aim.

"Someone asked for me last night?" Meg inquired, apologetically.

"The night manager at the marina office had a message for you; he may still be there." Meg's eyes got large and her heart skipped a beat, and she grabbed her stuff and headed out the door and over to the marina office.

"Are you staying another night?" he asked, but she didn't know.

At the marina office, Meg waited in line behind a few others who were checking in, checking out, and asking questions. They spoke Spanish, a lot of which she could understand. When her turn came, she introduced herself to the man at the counter and asked about the message. Yes, a message from *Moet*.

"In Ponce. Leaving today for Charlotte Amalie, Saint Thomas." The message continued, "Can she fly there?"

Was that all? Meg stood and questioned the note. She'd assumed Tom would have waited for her in Ponce or returned to Punta Cana. And he'd left no cell number for her to call. Perhaps he didn't know it was her. Maybe it was not Tom at all.

CHAPTER ELEVEN

German's Dilemma

Tomas's ultimatum did not sit well with German. He had no intention of taking Tomas to Havana. Not used to taking orders from crew members, especially a hitchhiker, he told Mariana so.

"It is my decision as captain to continue on to Tobago. You are wrong if you think I am going to Cuba. Put him on a plane tomorrow and tell him goodbye."

Mariana's hard side listened to German's words. Her soft side won.

"I'll talk to him again. He's just upset about all this news. He doesn't remember."

"Mariana, you think I don't know you want him for yourself?"

German walked off from Mariana. She kept an eye on him through the port-side window while he paced the deck in a huff. His plan to confuse and control Mariana had deteriorated in a matter of weeks. If Mariana came to realize the events of the night Max and Camilla left *Moet,* that German had lied to her, German might end up on the outside looking in. His balding head dripped perspiration into eyes filled with bright-red spider veins. The wind swept his long strands of comb-over hair straight in the air as he wiped the sweat from his forehead with his finger. His eyes still burned but not as much as his heart's hatred for Tomas.

It had surprised German when he got the message from the Punta Cana marina that Meghan Trumbo had called for him. How did she know where to find them? Maybe the news article? To put her off, German left the message for Meg, to meet up with them in Charlotte Amalie, Saint Thomas. They'd be long gone. By that time, his decision would be made on what to do with Tomas.

Hulia called Mariana. She would return to *Moet* after lunch. They'd have dinner together, spend the night aboard, and talk before she went home to Miami the next day. The sound of Hulia's voice made Mariana cry.

"Please, Hulie, can you come now? I told Tomas what I knew, and now he won't talk to me. And German knows, and he is acting strangely. I am frightened."

"Did you call Hymie first?" Hulia asked.

"No, I wanted to wait for you, and then I decided it would be best to tell Tomas the truth; I guess it's a mistake."

Hulia agreed, got her stuff together, canceled lunch with Rory, and returned promptly to the boat. Before Hulia arrived, German informed Mariana.

"We are leaving Ponce tonight for Sint Maarten. If you don't like it, call the police." When German blurted out his orders, Mariana stamped her foot one time to silence him, but he'd made up his mind. German was taking control. What would this night hold for them all?

Tomas was not cooking. He'd made himself scarce since she told him her news. German was not taking him to Havana. Tomas didn't have enough cash for an airline ticket and didn't own a credit card, and the false identification he carried in his pocket worried him. Tomas realized that he shouldn't have made threats when he had no options. His sketchy memory kept him a prisoner on *Moet* for now. Tom thought long and hard about it, but didn't remember the couple in the photo. He may have acted rashly. Maybe Mariana stood in his camp after all. Perhaps Mariana could help him get to Havana for some answers.

When Hulia arrived, Mariana poured a glass of wine for each of them, and since neither had had a bite to eat, she prepared an antipasto plate for them to share. They took it out to the balcony off Mariana's suite, a spot where they could talk privately. Initially, Hulia rambled on about Rory. Hulia always wandered off on a limb of a tree when a story was told.

"We had a lovely evening. He likes to talk about himself a lot. He has done a lot of interesting things. Been married twice and has one son, who is a hairdresser. Rory wants to come to Miami to visit me this fall after the weather breaks. I could deal with that, I think." Mariana listened and waited for her turn. "Actually, it ended up being a pity party for Rory." Then Hulia smiled. "He does own a high-tech helicopter. But he's such a bore." She was rolling her big brown eyes when she said the word *bore*.

When it was Mariana's turn, she began by talking about Max, not Tomas or German. She reminisced how he had come to her broke when Mariana married him. He carried schemes to get rich around with him in his head that needed to be funded by Mariana's money. They usually went sour. You could pick the man out in a crowd. The guy with "son of a bitch" written across his face. He had bushy blond hair and pearly white teeth too big for his mouth. He regularly sported a New York Yankees baseball cap and brightly colored gym shoes. His feet were big. These were shortcomings Mariana tolerated. She would not condone cheating. They'd had good times over the years before Mariana's drinking and drugging got the better of her and Max went awry.

Mariana began backtracking to Hulia. "About a month before we found Tomas and the dog, Max and I had a good dinner that Camilla prepared for us," Mariana said with disgust. "I can hardly even utter her name. I thought things were going good. We had delicious pecorino cheese and honey and a spicy sausage appetizer. After dinner, Max and I enjoyed a glass of port. You know, Hulie, a peaceful evening on the water, one of those nights to be on the boat. We drank and ate too much, and Max passed out in the cockpit. I went up to the upper deck and fell asleep up there."

Hulia already knew all about Max and that many of their nights had ended like this.

"I woke up and went to our suite. I think I remember that the door stood open, and as I approached, I could see Max and Camilla. Almost staged for me to see. Hulie, I went crazy. I began screaming, wailing, and calling out horrible names. Max pulled the revolver from the drawer next to the bed. I don't know if he planned to shoot me. Camilla woke up and pulled the covers up over her head. Then I grabbed the gun from Max, and it went off. Thank God, no one got shot. I threw a lamp against the bulkhead; I wanted to kill both of them. Then I ran off to be alone and forget."

Hulia held her hands to her head, shocked at what she'd heard. "Did you know anything about this? That they were having an affair?"

"I guess I saw the way he looked at her sometimes and then I would hear him playing with her in the galley."

"What do you mean, playing with her?"

"You know, teasing with her. Helping her cut up vegetables and making innuendos about how they might look like body parts and what he might like to do with them."

"Mar, Mar. Stop. It was right in front of you. Why didn't you end it and get rid of her. And of him, in your own time.

Mariana began feeling bad that Hulia was criticizing her.

"So then what happened?" Hulia asked.

"I don't remember what happened next, only that the next day, Max and Camilla were gone. Someone had made up the cabin, and German didn't speak of it. Then a few days later, German said he'd put them off on a raft. Hulie, I worried he'd killed them."

Hulia wondered. Was this the reason Hymie had asked her to arrange this last-minute visit? He wanted to know Mariana's story about Max and Camilla?

"Oh my God, Mariana, you need to call Hymie right now and tell him what you just told me. No, I am going to call him." Hulia selected the speed dial on her phone and repeated the story about Max and Camilla to Hymie. Then Hulia dropped the bomb about the night that *Moet* came upon Tomas, their new amnesiac crew member that they've kidnapped. The topping on the cake was German acting out and making threats to Mariana. Hymie didn't hesitate.

"All right, both you girls get your stuff together right now and get off that boat. Find yourself a safe place to stay and call me." And before he hung up, he asked Hulia, "So, where are the bodies? I assume in the sea?" With that question, Hulia's dry wit sprang out as usual.

"Well, Hymie, let's hope they're not in the trash compactor."

It brought a stern look from Mariana. Of course, Hymie knew that Max hadn't ended up adrift or in the compactor with Camilla; he had spoken to him after the incident. All of them, Hymie included, lived off Mariana and her corporation, and they all wore kid gloves when they dealt with her. Hulia was her only one true friend.

With the knowledge that German planned a midnight departure, Mariana packed more than essentials, and Hulia did the same. Chandon followed close behind her. She sensed more changes were to come for her, and she missed her mommy. Mariana scooped her up, and she laid her on the mat outside Tomas's cabin door. Then she and Hulia left and found a room at a nearby hotel away from the waterfront.

CHAPTER TWELVE

Determination

Had Meg been a fool? Had she read too much into the words of two sailors and gone off in hopes that Tom, the love of her life, had survived and boarded a fancy lady's luxury yacht? It sounded like a fantasy. All the people she met—Jhosep, Ann, Silvio, and the brothers in Havana—all wanted to be optimistic, but their eyes gave it away. They had to find something else to do, another place to look when they talked to her about it. A man surviving at sea for that many days was not probable. Only young Juan believed that Tom and Bitti could still be alive. She and Juan did. She once again questioned her mind, was she thinking like a child? Was Meg losing it?

Meg's intuition told her the message from *Moet* had not come from Tom. Going to Saint Thomas could be a long shot. Meg had come so far. To continue to Saint Thomas made sense to her. Someone on board that yacht had an answer for her. Why they might want to string her along, she didn't know. Whatever, and whoever, she needed to hear it from them.

At the taxi stand at the Punta Cana marina, Meg waited for her ride to the Punta Cana airport that had been called in for her by the hotel clerk. Forty minutes had passed. Meg walked to the office to check in with him.

"Didn't they show up?" he asked when he saw her.

"Maybe you could call again; I am hoping to get on a noon flight to Saint Thomas."

"Here, I have a break; I'll take you." He put a sign on the desk that said, "Back in an hour. Check in at the marina office."

He disappeared from the office while Meg waited outside on the stoop in front of the hotel. A rumble of straight pipes echoed through the streets of the complex. Meg's ears felt the sound coming closer and closer until it sat right there in front of her. The desk clerk, clad in a black leather jacket sat on the seat of an HD Sportster with an extended front end and a black tank painted with red lightning bolts.

"Come on. Get on."

Meg jumped on, and they pulled away down the long winding street of palms she came in on. She smiled to herself as she held onto E's waist and thought, when I find Tom, I sure got some stories for him.

The flight to Charlotte Amalie involved a connection in San Juan. The flight would bring her into Saint Thomas late that day. The Saint Thomas airport serviced the city of Charlotte Amalie and the other nearby islands. It was close to one of the piers where large yachts and cruise ships would be—and not too far from the downtown area and the main harbor where there would be more. The trip took less than an hour to San Juan, but then there was a six-hour layover before a brief flight into Saint Thomas.

Meg browsed the shops, bought a breakfast bar, and people watched. She asked an agent to recommend a restaurant she could cab to for lunch. On her way out, Meg passed a day spa that catered to travelers with extra time. TLC for You was the name. Although Meg was not a spa girl, she went in.

Her spa lady's name was Rose. She was an Asian woman, thin and ordinary and older, like Meg, but with long, straight black hair. While many Vietnamese immigrants born in the late sixties had American soldiers for fathers, she did not. The name on her license over her workstation was Linh—pronounced Lynn, meaning spirit or soul—Nguyen, the sir name pronounced Wing, although the ladies in the salon called her Rose. Born in Hanoi during the war, Rose had immigrated to Puerto Rico. She told Meg that Hanoi was now a big city, not like when she lived there. Meg tried to be polite, but when Rose asked her questions, Meg had to listen hard to understand her. Rose spoke Vietnamese English. Meg wanted to enjoy her massage, not talk. But somehow Rose sold her a hot stone therapy that Meg had never had before.

"You'll like it, you will see. I'll make it good for you, honey." She smiled. "You bring your man, and I will make it nice for the two of you; you will like it—I will show you. I give you two for one."

Meg didn't have the inclination or energy to explain about her man. When Rose continued to talk after a while, with close attention, Meg understood her perfectly. She spoke about the tragedy of the hurricane last year. How the area of San Juan, where she and her other neighbors lived, had suffered devastation. No electricity or water for a very long time.

The other girls talked about when they'd come to Puerto Rico. One chimed in that before she came to Puerto Rico, she'd lived in Nebraska. When she arrived there from Vietnam, she'd said to her sister, "What? This can't be America." And they all laughed, because they had expected to see an America that they read about in magazines. Flashy California girls and hot male models were not to be found in the flatlands of Nebraska.

They'd ended up in San Juan when an opportunity opened up to learn the art of massage therapy. The girls were not stupid, but they knew no one and could speak no English or Spanish. They found themselves being taken advantage of by men, even from their own country.

Meg nodded and agreed. As in the case of many immigrants in many cities, the Vietnamese congregated in the same area of San Juan. They helped each other. They spoke their native language, they watched each other's children, and they took in the elderly. They sang popular songs from American artists, and when they went out for the evening, they dressed sharp. They were westernized.

Rose spoke proudly of her position at the spa. After eight years, she had a long client list. Unfortunately, after Irma, traffic at the airport had stopped, and people that did visit didn't have time for a spa treatment. Most local people who were customers had left. People they knew got on cruise ships that offered free transport to Miami. For those that had lost everything and had no reason to stay, it made sense.

In the end, while Meg didn't rest much, Rose's chatter got her mind off her own problems. Meg saw that people everywhere were the same. Their troubles were foremost to them. They wanted a job, a home, and for their children to do better than they.

After Rose finished up, Meg still had time, so Rose sold her a mani-pedi. She made up a special that day, honey. All totaled, Meg chalked up nearly two hundred dollars plus a fifty dollar tip for Rose. It rejuvenated Meg, and when she boarded the Jet Blue flight to Charlotte Amalie, a handsome pilot at the Jetway gave her a wink. She thanked Rose for that.

Aboard, there were many tourists now beginning to vacation again in Puerto Rico and the Virgin Islands. The talk with the flight attendants said that Sint Maarten's economy struggled on all ends, both air traffic and cruises. The airport needed to be rebuilt, and the marinas on the Dutch side were laden with sunken boats and debris.

Barely off the ground, the captain announced their approach and the flight attendant asked the passengers to buckle up. The runway was so short that the landing was quick, with a firm brake. Everyone clapped except for Meg. She'd gotten over that years ago.

Meg remembered the large yacht dock as much closer. Her memory had failed her. She had to stop that, she said to herself. Unless you were a very aggressive walker with proper shoes, it would be too far, so Meg hailed a taxi. They drove by the beach that Tom and Meg played on with their big dog. The Old English sheepdog that they'd kept trimmed like a puppy. The breeder had docked her tail close to her backside, and it defined her bear-like gait. That dog ran so fast, with such strength, that her paws grabbed sand and threw it up in the air. Then, stopping short, she'd catch a disc in midair. She performed remarkable acrobatics to fetch it when Tom tossed it to her. The dog proudly reared up her head like a horse before she took a break and sat in the clear, shallow water to cool off. Her colossal pink tongue hung out the side of her mouth.

Meg stopped the driver and asked to get out.

"Please, this is fine. Drop me here."

A scattering of newly planted palm trees with wood braces set up the theater for Meg. Seagrass covered most of the beach. It made it narrower than before. It may have been the tide or the hurricane. She walked to the water, breathed in deeply, and picked up a fistful of sand. There were so many memories for her at that place. The ten years had gone by so fast. Meg held it up to her nose, and as she squeezed her fingers, the sand crumbled on the front of her shirt. The smell of the sea brought a bad taste to her mouth. Her stomach turned, and her lunch was at her throat, ready to spew out. Meg bent over. A strolling couple asked if she was ok. It brought her to her senses, and Meg threw the sand and wiped her palms on her shorts and nodded yes. She guessed the moment needed to happen.

Meg walked a half a mile farther around the next curve from where the taxi had dropped her. She saw the dock she remembered. She prayed she would find the motor yacht *Moet* waiting for her. A chain-link fence under lock and key enclosed the vacant area. The sign said, "Danger! Keep out!"

Meg went into the empty dockmaster's office. She needed to get a room and the status of the cruise ship dock area in downtown Charlotte Amalie. At the current location, there used to be a gourmet grocery store for provisioning, nice showers, and heads to accommodate boat owners who came for the weekend from Puerto Rico. Hurricane Irma had destroyed it.

Meg remembered a trawler in slip number one in 2008. When they spent time there, Meg had gotten to briefly know one of the liveaboards. This particular boat near them had left the States five years previous. The couple had a dream to live aboard and travel the islands together. Snorkel and dive the waters, revel in their youthful bodies, and live in paradise. Shortly after, the couple ran out of money, and the boat wouldn't run, so they sat in the slip permanently. The woman got a job, and her husband sat inside all day with the dog watching cable TV and drinking. When Meg walked by with her big dog in the evening to the grassy dog-walk area, Meg had seen her sitting in their cockpit alone, puffing cigarette after cigarette with her back to the sunset. Her name was Tammy. Her skinny, sun-scorched, wrinkled body had shown the toll life had taken on her. In the shadows, she appeared old, but in the daylight, Meg judged her for forty. Life had used her all up. They would shoot "good nights" to each other when Meg passed by. Other than that, they said nothing.

Tom had said it must suck to be Tammy.

The walk to the downtown harbor in the center of Charlotte Amalie took twenty minutes. The short trek took Meg on the cracked concrete sidewalks that buckled up from the surge and covered in rubble from the storm. A woman on the way recommended Nancy's Fancy, a newly remodeled hotel on the water open for business. The narrow yellow stucco building stood two stories high. Dark-brown cedar planks jetted out under the roofline. The grounds were well kept and had newly laid sod on the slopes in the front and the rear. From Meg's front balcony room, she had a view of boats anchored in the water and others tied at the docks. When she got to her room, she watched a seaplane landing in the harbor. Her room was immaculate, but when she peered out the windows away from the water, garbage and destruction lay everywhere. Roofs and sides of homes, small boats, trees, and cars piled up the mountainside like they'd been swept up there with a broom and left where they lay. Despite travel agent's reports, Saint Thomas was not in shape to do business. The first thing on Meg's list said to call the US Coast Guard Station San Juan to find out if they had any information on the motor yacht *Moet*. Hindsight told Meg she should have done that before flying to Saint Thomas.

CHAPTER THIRTEEN

German Makes His Move

Hulia called Rory when she and Mariana were ready to leave *Moet*, and he sent a crew member to pick them up and bring them to shore. Antonio watched and scrutinized the women disembarking with their bags. As the hours passed, German's attitude toward Tomas spiraled downward. His mind contemplated scary things. German believed he'd earned the right to sleep in Mariana's bed. Then this Tom Trumbo had come along.

"How could I be so unlucky to see this guy and his dog in the water that night? Me being a nice guy when I should have kept my mouth shut and let them float on by."

No moon lit up the water, and no stars lit the sky in the harbor that night. German pushed the button on the windlass and hoisted the anchor. It came up swift and clean and locked into place. The grinding noise of the chain at the bow tipped off Antonio and Tomas that they were leaving. The generators were pulsating, and German put the engines in gear. He spun *Moet* and hastily wove a path through the other boats at anchor. Before long, *Moet*'s lights could no longer be seen from the yacht club.

Antonio stayed silent. It was not right to him that Mariana was not onboard.

The GPS screen informed them of the distance. Two hundred thirty-two miles lay between Ponce and Sint Maarten. The course German set took them east of Puerto Rico and then directly into the westerlies toward Saint Thomas. The anemometer reported fifteen miles per hour. When they got near the coast of Saint Thomas, *Moet*'s course would continue east to Sint Maarten. The second leg always guaranteed a rough ride. For sailboats, the wind was a gift that pushed and pulled their boats steadily forward. They would hear the wind as they tacked left, then right. Yachts like *Moet* powered by diesel engines found those winds made their trip more difficult at times. It slowed them down and made their trip longer.

Antonio came up to the helm dressed in a T-shirt and shorts. German didn't like his outfit and had a puss.

"Ca-ca-ca-ca-pitán, Ms. Mariana and her friend are gone. What does it matter what I wear?"

Antonio caught German by surprise, and German returned questioning eyes. German did not want to admit that he did not know Hulia and Mariana were gone. So he made it up.

"They will join us in Sint Maarten," German responded coolly to hide his concerns. The truth be known, German had lost control of Mariana. He consoled himself. "This is probably better with Mariana not aboard; now I can make my own decisions about Tomas." That news added more stress. German captained *Moet*, but he was out of control.

Tomas showed up on the bridge with Chandon. Disgusted with him, German said, "If you have nothing to do, why don't you make us some food?"

"No problem, I can do that. Will Hulia and Mariana be eating? It's pretty late."

"They are not aboard. The two are meeting us in Sint Maarten." German blurted it out as a matter of fact. Tomas's expression showed surprise and concern. He comprehended that with Mariana gone, *Moet* could be a dangerous place for him to be.

He took the dog to the galley with him, made sandwiches, and then took them up to the bridge. When he got there, Antonio and German were talking about one of the engines. Being an experienced second mate and diesel engineer, Antonio had rules and guidelines regarding repair schedules. If there was a question, he just wouldn't push it. Mariana had given him the authority to overrule German. That night if he were able to make the call, they wouldn't be out there in the dark with one faulty engine.

German slammed his fist on the helm and screamed at Antonio. "Well, if we had a problem with an engine, I would expect our diesel specialist would have fixed it."

Antonio would not argue. He stood up for himself. "I got the part I needed today. I wasn't expecting to take off in the middle of the night and take chances before I completed the repair. You know, we don't want to end up out here in this wind, in the dark, on one engine."

German knew it too, and after they traveled about a hundred miles and were just off the coast of Saint Thomas, the port engine began to overheat. The display numbers rose, and Antonio went to the engine room. He returned to report that they needed to shut down the port engine and continue on one engine if they were going all the way to Sint Maarten that night. Alternatively, he recommended they should go into Charlotte Amalie harbor in Saint Thomas now.

German screwed up his face and objected. In his mind, going into Saint Thomas and taking a chance to run into Tomas's wife was not acceptable to him. All this might come back to haunt him.

"We'll keep both engines running and continue to Sint Maarten as planned. If we have a problem, then we can turn back."

Against his better judgment, Antonio did what German told him. Then German passed the helm over to Antonio, and he went to his cabin.

"This could probably damage the engine. Couldn't it?" Tomas questioned Antonio.

"Yes, it could and probably will and may already have. I may have to make my own decision and take over."

A nervy statement coming from Antonio's mouth. One he'd never had to make before or even consider. Poor Antonio couldn't even get the word *captain* out of his mouth in one try, let alone take over the captain's job. Antonio had to put a plan together and act fast.

German came out of his cabin and called to Tomas to come to help him below. German called to him in the dark from the stern.

"Ok, this is the end of the road—into the water with you." And he pointed a handgun at Tom.

Tomas's body stood shocked. He'd known German might be a bad guy, but he'd never expected this.

Tomas had about enough. "If you want me in the water, you'll have to shoot me." Tomas responded, and he started to turn away.

Bang! The sound of German's weapon snapped in the air. He may have meant to scare him, but the bullet grazed his shoulder. It caught Tomas off balance, and he fell backward into the water. Disorientated, he struggled to surface and tread water. German slid the gun into his belt and returned to the helm. His ruthless mind had no remorse. German had solved his problem. He pushed the throttles forward, and *Moet* pulled away.

Tomas was treading shark-infested waters. His wound leaked tinges of bright-red blood, and it floated around his body. The little dog stood in the shadow on the swim platform, where there lay a long coiled line tied to a Jim-Buoy life ring. They'd trained her on *Tori's Seacret*, and she nudged it off, and the line stretched out into the water. Tomas slipped his good arm into the ring. He had saved the dog once, and now it was her turn. Once Bitti witnessed Tomas's body dragging behind, she stood watch and waited.

Earlier that night, Mariana and Hulia had sat in Hulia's hotel room in Ponce with a bottle of red wine and a decadent cheese and fruit plate. They both wore the imported silk kimonos they'd bought shopping in Ponce.

"Ok," Hulia said. "Before we drink too much, it's time to call Hymie."

"What if we just let things be? Let German take the boat wherever he chooses. I can cancel my credit cards, and he'll run out of money and have to leave the boat someplace. I'll probably never hear from him again."

"Whoa, wait a minute, girlfriend, it's not just about you. I'm involved in this too. German is a bad guy. Who knows what he will do. I have no family, but you have to think of your daughter. Where did you find this German, anyway?"

"Max hired him; he liked him because he did things for him." Again Hulia rolled her big brown eyes as she took a taste of the wine.

"I love you, Mar, but you got bad luck with men. And there's nothing that's going to convince me that the Max-and-his-girlfriend episode wasn't a setup. The whole thing sounded made up. What were you taking that night, anyway?"

"Nothing! Nothing that I don't normally take. Max took care of me." She picked up the cell phone and gave it to Mariana. "Call Hymie." Hymie answered immediately and enabled the speaker.

"Ok, so, how are you girls doing tonight? Did you follow my instructions?" Hulia could hear his voice, and she pictured his small, thin body—and a mustache too large for his face—sitting at a desk also too big, an antique that had belonged to his father and his father's father before him. Hymie had come into his own. He'd studied abroad, gotten his law degree in Chicago and his doctorate in New York, and argued before the US Supreme Court. He'd majored in taxes, trusts, and wills. When Hulia's family died, Hymie had managed the estates. He was a rough and gruff man who didn't sound like the slight man sitting at the other end of the phone. The bad guys he called "pigs," and he would tell his clients when they had to deal with one.

"Fuck 'em!"

"Yes, Hymie," Mariana answered. "We got off the boat with our stuff, and we got rooms in Ponce."

"Ok, first thing, I've been thinking about this situation with Max and Camilla. Is your mate Antonio involved in any of this?" he asked Mariana.

"I don't remember him being involved, but lots of times, I don't remember when I drink. I assumed he was asleep or at the helm since German was there."

"So no witnesses. It is just your word against German's about what occurred. Where did Antonio think Max and the cook went, and where exactly did they end up?"

"I don't know all the facts. German said he put them on a raft. I have no idea what Antonio thought. It was never talked about."

"I am not a divorce lawyer, Mariana, but this incident could complicate divorce proceedings, because you have knowledge of the incident. We don't know if, actually, a crime occurred or if it could show abuse on your part. German as captain has the right to put Max and the cook off the boat. But endangering their lives on a raft could be construed as attempted murder." Then Hymie paused. "First, we need to deal with German. I think you need to contact the authorities as well as the coast guard and report the yacht stolen. You will tell them that you and Hulia went ashore and returned and found it gone. In the morning, call and talk to the yacht club dockmaster there and tell him you reported the boat missing. Cancel your credit cards, and we will see where this all takes us. Can you deal with this, Mariana?"

"The dockmaster is a friend of German's. He might call him; what if…" Mariana started to squirm.

"Mariana," Hymie scolded her. "The boat is missing. That's all you know. The dockmaster is not going to get involved with a guy who steals yachts. Tomorrow, I will talk to my colleague about all this and what to do with this Tomas fellow you picked up along the way." Then he paused again. "Jeez Louise, Mariana! Kidnapping? Putting your husband overboard? Your grandma and grandpa," he said in Spanish. "God rest their souls; they would be screaming at me."

They ended their conversation. In the morning, Mariana called the coast guard and reported the theft.

It was the early morning of July 9. Meg lay facedown on her pillow in her bed at Nancy's Fancy hovering over Charlotte Amalie harbor. Tomas dangled on a line behind *Moet* not far offshore, Angeli hid away shivering in the crew quarters, and Antonio contemplated mutiny.

An engine alarm went off on *Moet*'s helm station. Antonio shut down the port engine, and *Moet*'s speed slowed. Antonio reported to German that they had no choice but to go into Saint Thomas immediately. As they came into the harbor at Charlotte Amalie, the rising sun outlined the clouds in front of them. German called the harbormaster repeatedly and finally got an answer. The morning dew made *Moet*'s deck wet and slippery. Antonio carefully began to untie the lines and attached them to the cleats for docking. He hadn't seen Tomas in a while. German at the helm witnessed a welcoming committee of two US Coast Guard cutters off the port. Antonio could see them also. The cutter captain hailed *Moet* on the radio, while another guardsman called out to them on a loudspeaker. Every boat moored in the harbor switched on their lights.

"Motor yacht *Moet*," the cutter captain called.

"Yes, this is *Moet*," German answered.

"Request permission to come aboard, Captain."

"Ca-ca-ca-ca-pitán. What's going on?" Antonio asked. He knew from his own experience that the coast guard might board you in US waters. But here in the harbor, it seemed odd to him.

"Just do as they say, and everything will be ok." German had no patience with his mate.

They came alongside, four of them. Two coast guard officers climbed up to the helm with them and asked the captain to identify himself.

"I am the captain," German said as he handed over his passport and boat documentation, which he'd pulled out of a drawer in the bridge. One guardsman stayed with German as the others searched the vessel.

"Last port? And where are you going?"

"We left Ponce during the night heading for Sint Maarten, when an engine failed. The owner is meeting us there."

"How many passengers and crew on board, Captain?"

German replied, "Just the two of us, sir." Antonio heard his lie but kept quiet.

"Do you know the owner has reported the vessel as stolen?"

"No, sir; last I talked to her, she directed that I go to Sint Maarten and wait for her and her friend to meet us there. That was last night in Ponce."

"Well, Captain, my orders are to detain you and the vessel." They took German into custody and removed him and Antonio from the boat to a coast guard detention building on the harbor.

With *Moet* at the dock, Tomas followed the line and pulled himself up to the boat and climbed onto the swim platform. He felt weak and out of breath. He lay flat, and little Bitti cleaned the wound on his shoulder with her healing saliva. Soon after, when Angeli saw the coast was clear and German gone, Angeli crept out of her hiding place and helped Tomas into his cabin and dressed his wound.

CHAPTER FOURTEEN

Antonio's View

Antonio waited in his cell at the detention center, hoping to be released. No one asked him any questions. His eyes lacked sleep, and he shook from the strong coffee they gave him on an empty stomach. He reflected on the things he'd seen on *Moet* while he worked for Max and Mariana. He reflected on the night before—and the days before that and the weeks before that, to the last night he'd seen Max and Camilla. He had been in his bunk when he heard Camilla outside the crew quarters talking on her phone. She giggled and whispered, making plans. She chatted with Mariana's husband, Max.

Camilla had been hired on, like he, by German after he became captain. She was a young French girl with short blond hair that she wore swept to the side over her eyes like a boy. Cute and sweet, with her accent and her large black outlined eyes and slim body. Antonio couldn't blame Max at all. The three of them—German, Antonio, and Camilla—had spent time all over the Caribbean and Mexico years earlier. Antonio had shared a bunk with Camilla a few times too. He found her as creative there as in the galley. Camilla was also a capable shipmate. She could handle lines, polish the outside of the boat, and do laundry. He didn't know too much about her past; she was private. But he did witness her ability up in the helm helping German setting courses and contacting marinas for reservations and information on approach information.

During his time, Antonio had also witnessed several disagreements between Max and Mariana as a result of Mariana's jealousy. German had seen
it too. For Antonio, working aboard *Moet* entailed much more than being
an engine mechanic. He had to be that and the first mate, maintenance
man, friend, protector, and psychologist to everyone aboard.

The door burst open and closed with a crash. The guard carried in
lunch. The noise brought Antonio to the present, and it made him think of
Angeli. During the excitement, he hadn't seen her leave the boat in Ponce,
and he hadn't seen her on board yesterday. Angeli kept out of the way when
she worked. Most of the time, she worked in the very early mornings while
everyone slept. Angeli worked in the laundry room at all hours in the laza-
rette at the stern out of sight. Antonio didn't know about Angeli any more
than he knew about Tom. And he was angry with himself.

German sat in the cell next to Antonio. There were no bars between
them but a solid wall that kept them from seeing each other, but they could
talk. German couldn't sit still, and Antonio could hear German's left shoe
squeak and click as he paced. Mariana had betrayed him, and German
couldn't imagine what she'd told the authorities about him. Why did she
need to say the boat had been stolen? He called out to Antonio.

"Antonio, bud, they say Mariana reported the boat missing last night.
Why do you think she said that? She told me to meet her in Sint Maarten."
German wanted to firm up in Antonio's mind how he saw Mariana's orders.
So when the authorities ask him, Antonio would follow his lead.

Antonio responded, "I don't know. Things didn't seem right, us leaving
them behind. We've never done that before. And I hadn't seen Angeli all
night or Tomas either."

German's shoe immediately stopped squeaking, and the two holes in his
head bugged open wide with disbelief. More problems for German. German
knew what happened to Tomas, but Angeli, he didn't know. Could she have
seen him when he forced Tomas off the boat with the gun? She might be a
witness. Her testimony could send him to prison for murder.

Just after nine that morning, Mariana received a call from the coast guard in San Juan. They reported *Moet* tied at the dock in Charlotte Amalie Harbor in Saint Thomas. It had limped in on one engine before dawn and been boarded by four guardsmen on two cutters. The captain and mate, German and Antonio, were being detained.

"There were four aboard and a little dog," Mariana stated. "Where are they?"

"Your captain reported only two aboard, ma'am. And our search proved it to be true. The captain and mate are here at the detention center. Do you want to press charges, ma'am?"

"I want you to hold them until I talk with my attorney for advice. Can you do that for me?"

"Yes, but only till three o'clock. If there's been a mistake and the crew has done nothing wrong, I will need to follow the procedure. Your crew has rights. This is only out of courtesy to you as the vessel owner that I will hold them without being charged."

"Thank you; I will be in touch with you well before that time."

Immediately, she called Hymie and reported the news as Hulia listened in. Hulia sat at a table eating a Belgian waffle with strawberries and peaks of stiff whipped cream. She slathered it with butter with her knife and carefully poured the maple syrup until it filled every square. The sight of it made Mariana gag.

"Tell me what you want to do, Mariana, arrest the guy for grand theft and have him deported to Mexico? That could be a death sentence for him," Hymie added.

"Well, at least I would know where he was. My other options are to cut him loose, hire a new captain, or have Antonio continue the trip to Tobago for the hurricane season. I can't keep German. There are too many questions about him. Who knows what he might do."

"If you want to prosecute him, I can call over there and get things in motion. And Mariana, it is what it is; there are too many people involved now. You may have no choices in the matter."

Hymie noticed and was glad to hear that Mariana appeared very much in control of herself during their conversation. No weakness in her voice.

No sounds from a poor woman being taken advantage of, at least not today. She must have been sober.

"I am feeling bad about Tomas and the dog and the cleaning lady." Mariana wasn't even sure of her name. "They are all innocent victims involved in a bad situation. I think I want to go there and talk to Antonio to see how he's feeling and get answers before I make my decision."

"They're not going to hold German much longer without charging him."

"Well, if you could call the coast guard, and talk to them, we have a friend here with a helicopter that would probably fly us there this afternoon." Hulia nodded at Mariana when she said that.

"Ok, Mariana, if that's what you want to do, you get there as soon as you can, and I'll call them."

Hulia got on her phone to call Rory, the owner of the Pershing. A guy with nothing to do and ready to go at a moment's notice. He loved the idea of taking Mariana and Hulia to Saint Thomas and showing off his helicopter. He'd call his pilot and get a time frame for departure.

"Hulie, will you go with me?" Mariana pleaded with Hulia. "I know you had planned to go home today, but if you could go with me, I need your support. I am frightened." Hulia loved Mariana for all the things she did for her and the special times they shared.

"I will help you any way I can, Mar. I just don't know if I will really be an asset."

"Just be there for me, Hulie. For nothing else but to be a witness."

The differences between Hulia and Mariana were night and day. Mariana spoke slowly, and low, and because of that, people listened attentively when she spoke. Like she had a secret to share with them. Hulia spoke loudly, and her voice's pitch went up like scales played on a piano keyboard. When Hulia spoke, people also listened but more because of the way she entered the room like a band at a parade. They listened because they had no choice. Mariana remained silent, waiting for Hulia to answer. She didn't have to wait long; Hulia's expression said it all. Hulia gave her a hug. Hulia wiped the remains of the syrup from her mouth, applied a fresh coat of creamy red lipstick in the mirror, and canceled her flight to Miami.

When the American Airlines jet went down in the nineties, the authorities had searched for survivors. Mariana had waited with Hulia's parents. Although the plane was located promptly after, four survivors were separated from the aircraft and found a ways from the carnage. Hulia's parents were beside themselves. The finality of death touched them. With all their money, nothing separated their family riding in the first-class seats from those riding in economy. They cried and consoled strangers. Watching and waiting, they were all lost souls, in a fog, waiting for a miracle. And then a miracle happened. They found Hulia alive.

Mariana would never forget, as the spokesperson for Hulia's family, what it was like—first, the discovery of Hulia and then the discovery of her husband's and children's bodies. Mariana had broken the news and told Hulia before her parents came into her room. And then she'd left so they could mourn alone to hold their only child. Afterward, a long period of both physical and mental rehabilitation ensued for Hulia and her parents.

The helicopter ride to Saint Thomas took more time than Mariana expected. They wore headphones, and Rory did a lot of talking and pointing to Hulia as they passed over different sights. The view from the helicopter was much better than from a plane, and as they flew and Hulia and Rory talked, Mariana removed her phones to get away from the chatter to think.

At the airport, they agreed that Rory would wait for them for word before leaving. Mariana and Hulia got a taxi ride to the harbor, where Mariana wanted to go first to board *Moet* for a look-see before talking with anyone. She stopped at the marina office to give her ID, and the manager accompanied her and Hulia to the dock and to *Moet*.

When she approached the boat, she saw it like she rarely had before. Filthy from the trip. Covered in salt and black soot spewed along the hull near the exhaust. Mariana knew enough about the boat to understand that it probably had to do with running on one engine and at such a slow speed. That mess would have usually been cleaned up long before she ever saw it, but the nature of its arrival that morning left no time for that. The manager accompanied the two women aboard and walked with them through the boat, well aware of the episode of arrival and the removal of the crew by the coast guard. Everyone on the docks and the sailboaters moored in the harbor knew the details. They were gossiping and asking questions after being awakened by the noise of the speakers from the coast guard cutters. Big news for a little harbor.

Mariana walked through the entire boat and found nothing out of the ordinary. The galley was clean, although the compacter would always leave her with a disgusting recollection. She moved on quickly. All the heads had fresh towels. Her housekeeper had definitely been there. Mariana walked up to the bow and then to the cockpit and down the stairs to the swim platform and saw nothing. She heard the humming sound of the generator from the water sloshing and chugging. As Mariana turned to leave, she heard a sound from the compartment door to the crew's quarters. She pulled it open. She saw Bitti, Angeli filled with fear, and Tomas lying in the bunk. It was the second time Mariana had seen him that way and the second time she would come to his aid and save his life.

CHAPTER FIFTEEN

Things Left Unsaid

Meg stood by the window of her modest room at the busy harbor in Saint Thomas, sipping a cup of black coffee. Most of the boats were moored. They were sailboats and trawlers, and a cargo ship wedged in on the far side of the marina. The larger boats tied at the docks in view were not large enough to be the motor yacht *Moet*.

Over the past twelve days, she had worked hard to keep calm and be patient.

"Patience is a virtue," her mother-in-law had told her. She'd learned that to be true. Patience had helped her keep control to bring her this far.

Meg finished dressing and put on her makeup, but just before she finished, she heard a knock at her door.

"Housekeeping."

Meg acknowledged and moved out onto a small balcony. She sat on a sky-blue Adirondack chair shaded by a yellow-and-white flowering frangipani tree. In Hawaii, the flowers were used to make leis for the tourists. Meg breathed in the sweet fragrance while she waited for the housekeeping staff to make up her room. Meg thought about Jhosep. How lucky that he'd stood by her and gotten her to Havana, where she'd needed to be to meet the two sailors who spoke of Luperón and the little white dog. Jhosep didn't have to do that. Then Ann and Silvio offered their hospitality. And little Juan, a little boy, gave her the confidence that she would find Tom. That led Meg's thoughts to Luperón and then Punta Cana to those who lent a hand or kind word, for free, to an American woman alone in their country.

Then Meg reconsidered the message from the unknown caller at the Punta Cana marina. Someone aboard the motor yacht *Moet* knew about her and Tom. That wasn't her hunch or intuition or hope. It was a fact. Tom had survived in the water, and recently he had been alive. Meg assured herself that, on that day, she'd find Tom or know his fate.

Meg went in person to the coast guard station in the harbor instead of calling. Better to go in person to get the answers she needed. But the officer in charge had business in San Juan and would return after lunch.

Humph! Better she should have called.

Rather than sit and wait all that time, Meg went to her room and planned to return after lunch. She had to eat. She made a call home and then a call to Ann in Havana. In Saint Thomas, her cell phone worked like in the States. Ann gave her the news that Jhosep had moved in with them and was recovering. Ann told Meg that the dockmaster at Hemingway Marina had found a man to watch the boat, start its engines, and rinse it off. It concerned Meg that she didn't know him, but she had no choice.

Meg found a restaurant at a hotel a few streets above the harbor behind the shopping area. The building that housed the café had barely survived Hurricanes Maria and Irma. A blue tarp covered the missing wood planks on the restaurant's roof, and bamboo reeds tied together covered the bar. Tropical foliage rebounded quickly and acted as camouflage for the hidden damage that still existed. Already many of the large trees that were stripped of their leaves were sprouting new ones. The hostess poured red grapefruit sangria in large glasses. The restaurant served a buffet of salads and fresh seafood. Meg only had one glass, tasting overly sweet, and she remembered why she didn't like sangria.

Meg thought about the Keys during Hurricane Irma in September 2017. The week they'd lost their bobtail. A heart attack had taken her. She had been old for a big dog but had pranced on the dock with friends a few days before. She'd lay on *Tori's Seacret*'s galley floor, panting heavily, and Meg laid with her and stroked her head. Matey had raised her head with a jolt and let out a feeble squeal and flopped her head hard on the floor.

Meg had called out to Tom. "It's Matey."

"No…" He cupped his hand gently on her heart. He felt no rhythm or beats. She had already left them. He closed her eyes with his fingers and used a blanket to cradle her body. Meg put a white *Tori's Seacret* T-shirt over her head and eased it onto her body. Tom pulled anchor and drove out to the deepest and clearest waters of the Gulf Stream. Meg set her body free as gently as she could through the tuna door and watched her body float along. The current moved fast, between five and six knots. Tom and Meg saw it grab her body away from the boat. They drifted with her for a while as the current built distance between them. Her dead weight left the surface, and she disappeared. Then Tom and Meg went up to the helm, and he blasted the horn three long times. Huuuuh…huuuuh…huuuuh. Meg had forgotten how loud and deep the sound could be. Meg's eyes tried to mark the spot until she could no longer see where they'd left her. She had given them thirteen loyal years.

Alone at her table in Saint Thomas, Meg looked at her food like a sad sack. She asked herself. Why do people need to punish themselves like that? Her watch said twelve thirty. She wiped her eyes, paid her bill, and walked down the hill to the coast guard office.

On her way, she noticed she'd left her wedding band behind in her room. It must have been when housekeeping interrupted her dressing and she stepped out on the patio. She damned herself and swore to remember to look for it. The thought that it might be a sign of the results of her gene test left her head immediately. She had no time for that. On the street that encircled the harbor, an ambulance wined and sped by as she waited to cross. Once in the building and at the reception window, Meg once more asked to see the officer in charge. The reception officer assured her that he had been detained but would be there shortly. Meg took a seat in the large red-and-white tiled lobby area near the window, where she watched a scene in the harbor. She focused on a big yacht at the end of the dock. One big enough to be the yacht, *Moet*. The ambulance pulled up there, and emergency personnel swarmed all around it. Meg's heart skipped. While Meg watched the dock, an officer came into the building, walking quickly right by her into an office. Two well-dressed women and a brown-skinned woman with a baby wrapped in a blanket followed behind him. Mariana, Hulia, and then Angeli. The office door slammed closed.

At the reception window, Meg inquired again anxiously. "Is that the officer that I am waiting for?"

"Yes, I know you were here before, but he got busy on the telephone, and now he's handling an emergency. You need to wait. He knows you are here." He patronized her, but she saw he had no control. Meg took a card from her bag, a *Tori's Seacret* business card, and she passed it to him through his window.

"This is me, Meg Trumbo." And she returned to her seat.

The office door opened, and Meg watched as two of the women came out accompanied by the officer. He unlocked an *Employees Only* door at the other side of the room, and they went in.

Once inside, Mariana began trembling at the idea of confronting German. She walked up to the cell that held Antonio first. No words were spoken. She put her finger up to her lips and passed him a note that read, "I know the truth. Angeli is here, and Tomas is safe. You have no worries from me." As Antonio read the note, his eyes responded to Mariana with relief. He sat and listened while Mariana moved in front of German's cell. Hulia stood tall and firm next to Mariana, holding her forearm.

When German saw Mariana before him, he remained quiet, waiting to hear what she had to say to him. His form stood humbled and relayed his bewilderment about her actions the night before.

"Sir," Mariana said to the officer, "you can leave us alone now. And please let Antonio out of that cage." Antonio fell forward in relief.

"Just press the button when you are finished," the officer responded.

Mariana hadn't even begun speaking to German when his expression went from humility to rage as he lunged at the bars. She and Hulia stepped back.

"I have seen and have talked with Angeli; she is with me here in the office. I found her with Tomas in the stern of the boat. Luckily for you, he is alive."

His twisted face glared at her, and the next words spat out of his mouth. "You can't listen to Angeli. She is nothing but a pregnant bitch. You didn't know that, did you? What did she say about me?"

"What are you talking about? She didn't need to say anything. I found her, and I saw."

A period of silence followed before German spoke. "I have been loyal to you. I watched out for you. I saved you from embarrassment many times. Things you don't even remember. You owe me, Mariana."

Hulia's ears burned at what she heard. She felt an urge to punch German in the nose to defend Mariana. She hunted for words but could not find them. Mariana moved closer to the cell and began to speak slowly and softly to him, hesitating after each word. Her message came out clear and precise. Mariana was not confused.

"I made promises to you, German, and I kept them. Not because you deserved it but because I made them. I told you that, after Max left, you could continue to be *Moet*'s captain as long as you acted according to my rules. You are no longer the captain of *Moet* because you broke them. I'll pay you six months' severance, and you'll sign a confession here, now. You are to return to Mexico immediately. I will pay for your transportation. I'll have the officer release you when that's done. That's the end. It's over."

"Confess to what? What am I going to confess to?" German screamed out at them as they filed out of the detention center.

"It will all be prepared for you, German; you just sign it. Don't fuck with me, German. There is no negotiating here." Gratification filled her, and Hymie came to mind when Mariana said it.

When they walked out the door, Hulia turned and slapped Mariana's palm.

"Woo-hoo! Girlfriend, I am proud. Of. You. Can I go home now?" Mariana laughed at her and slapped her arm. With that, the three of them—Mariana, Hulia, and Antonio—left the detention area. Mariana waited for Angeli and Chandon to join them from the office. When the officer's door opened, the little white dog darted across the room, whining, wiggling, and wagging all the way. She leapt up into Meg's lap. No second thoughts for any of them. This was Meg Trumbo.

Mariana and Hulia were shocked. Angeli stood confused. They met midway in the room. Meg held the dog, and Mariana led the others. Their eyes met, and Meg knew at once one of them had to be the fancy lady that the sailors had talked about in Havana. Mariana recognized Meg from the newsletter in Punta Cana. When Mariana and Meg came together, both hesitated. Things needed to be said, but neither one did. Hulia stepped forward and then embraced her, introducing herself. With that, Mariana broke up, shedding bogus crocodile tears, and the three of them hugged. No translation required.

The officer arranged for a taxi to take all of them, Angeli and Bitti included, to the hospital to see Tomas, a.k.a. Tom Trumbo. They all piled in.

CHAPTER SIXTEEN

Insults and Injury

The ride to the local hospital took them up a steep hill, too much for them to walk. Meg could have navigated it, but neither Mariana nor Hulia was wearing the proper shoes for it. Once out of the taxi, Meg had a hard time coming to grips with what had just happened and what may come next. Things had happened so quickly. She had expected to find Tom but not like this. Mariana didn't offer any explanation, and after all of her travels and anticipation, Meg had no words. What would he say? What would she say? It had been barely a few weeks. She questioned it because of the miles that were between them and the not knowing. How did Tom end up here in the hospital in Saint Thomas?

Meg stood outside the hospital room. Hulia saw her struggling and pitied her. Mariana took the lead as she had with Hulia when she lost her family and walked into his room while Meg's feet were glued to the floor in the hallway. The good news for all concerned, he was alive.

Mariana found relief in Tomas's eyes. He smiled when he saw her. He'd gotten over their confrontation over the newsletter. And he had forgiven her for hiding things from him. Tomas asked a lot of questions about the trip and the arrival in Saint Thomas, about Antonio, Angeli, and, of course, German. Trying to keep it all about business, he apologized to Mariana about the delay getting to Sint Maarten, and Mariana patted his hand to comfort him.

Before any more discussion, Meg entered the room, carrying Bitti. Tomas had no reason to expect that. No one had told him. Meg received a blank look when she laid the little dog next to him on the bed. Sadly for her, he didn't remember. He saw an attractive stranger with a cute figure and hair, but he did not recognize her. When she said, "Hi, stranger," with a sweet smile, she blushed, and Bitti climbed all over him and licked him vigorously and then Meg. An awkward reunion tried to take place in the room. No scripts were written for either of them. It was like a graduation reunion where no one remembers you. Meg wanted to leave. Tomas looked away from her out the window, and it became evident to everyone in the room, especially Meg, that she didn't belong. She imagined meeting in a field of daffodils, running in slow motion, with Bitti following behind, filled with glee. Then a long embrace and a movie star kiss that went on and on. But not there, not today.

Tomas's doctor entered. In a beautiful Indian accent, he reported to Tomas and Mariana, not Meg. He recommended that Tomas stay in the hospital until the following day. He wanted him to continue antibiotics for his wound and rest and regain his strength and combat his dehydration. He explained the simple care he needed to take and asked if he could remain in Saint Thomas for a week for a follow-up.

Tomas spoke up immediately. "No, I need to leave; I signed on for the trip to Tobago, that is, if they will wait for me. I can fly and meet up with them if you think I need to stay a little longer. But not a week."

Meg felt sick. No, she was devastated. She had the shakes. She wished she had the nerve to slap him. Meg wanted to take the flyer out of her pocket with their photo of their last night in Key West and point to it and say to him, "This is you, Tom; this is me, Meg, and this is Bitti. This is us. Thirty years of us."

Mariana's expression was ridden with malignant pleasure at the position that Meg found herself in. Mariana and Tomas both knew what had been going on.

Meg stood in a purgatorial trance, a place between heaven and hell or wherever you go when you die and walk into a room like a ghost, and no one sees you. She didn't say anything, just held her breath. She needed for her Tom to say, "I need to go with my wife to get our boat." Or for Mariana to say, "No, Tomas, I have another person lined up; you can go with Meg." But neither one did. Oh, my God. No one did. It became time then for Meg to speak up. She opened her mouth, but just like it had been all through her life, nothing came out. Meg just went along, following along, walking in his steps, living his life. She was upset, all right—not at him but at herself for being so weak. She thought she was strong, but for all the places that this recent journey had taken her, as soon as she saw her Tom, submissive Meg returned.

Conveniently for Tomas, his pain meds began to kick in, and he became drowsy and nodded off. It was time for everyone to leave the room, especially Meg, who tottered on an all-out breakdown. She needed time for regrouping, rethinking, and reevaluating what had just happened. She grabbed Bitti from the bed and led Mariana and the doctor out of the room as Mariana looked back and smiled over her shoulder at the patient in the bed.

"Tomas, you call me if you need anything," Mariana said.

Once out, Meg turned to Dr. Singh, as it read on his coat.

"I really want to talk to you. Do you have time for me?"

"I need to complete my rounds here in the hospital, but after that, if you come to my office at the clinic next door, I can see you at four o'clock."

She agreed. Meg had about an hour and a half to kill. Meg asked Mariana if she had a few minutes alone to talk. Mariana agreed, but first, she needed to ride to the airport with Hulia, where Rory and his copter waited. They set the plan that Meg and Mariana were to meet at the doctor's clinic waiting area at three thirty.

Tomas lay in the R. L. Schneider Hospital. It had been named after Roy Lester Schneider, who served as the fifth elected governor of the territory. During the Vietnam War, he'd served as a medical advisor and been awarded the Bronze Star by the United States. The hospital was located thirty-six feet above sea level from Charlotte Amalie Harbor. That salvaged it from the rising water. From the window, Tomas could see *Moet* sitting at the dock in the harbor.

Meg waited alone with Bitti on her lap outside Tomas's room until it was time to meet Mariana. The freshly painted walls and the new hardwood flooring of the hospital gave it a much-needed lift since she had seen it last. Meg had suffered an emergency gallbladder attack. The only surgeon capable of performing the surgery was on vacation in Saint John at a wedding. Meg had to wait until the doctor returned by boat to treat her. All went well, but it made her think what a tragedy it would have been if it occurred while they were at sea or anchored off a remote island. That's how people died from a treatable diagnosis.

Meg googled the names of lawyers in Charlotte Amalie. Tom had been in a terrible boating accident, lost at sea, had no recollection of his wife and his life. Yet she'd stood in his room like a ninny and gotten railroaded by this woman Mariana and this guy named Tomas.

How many days had it been since she spoke with Carol? Her daughter led a busy life, and so did Meg, and weeks could go by without conversation. She needed to call her. Carol saw "Mom" light up her screen and answered immediately.

"I wondered when you were going to call me," she scolded Meg. "I've called you three times, and it goes right into voice mail. Where are you, now?"

"I know. I know. I'm in Saint Thomas with good news. I saw your father today."

"Oh my God! That's wonderful, Mom. Why didn't you call sooner? Where has he been?"

"I got word that he was on a yacht that was coming here, so I flew here yesterday, and Dad's here in the hospital in Charlotte Amalie."

"Is he ok?" Carol's words tread softly and carefully.

"He's been through a lot. Most of which I don't even know about yet. But he's basically ok." Meg hesitated but not too long. "He doesn't remember."

"He doesn't remember what happened?"

"He doesn't remember anything. And he doesn't remember me."

"Oh. Mom." Carol's voice sent sympathy to her. "You have to get him home."

"Yes, I think so too. But I don't know if he will come." Meg knew what would follow. Her daughter, Carol, had Tom's personality and disposition.

"Mom, you have to take charge. For the first time in your life, you have to take charge." Then Carol hesitated and wanted to apologize, but the daughter-mother relationship wouldn't let her.

"Carol, you don't understand what's going on here."

"I guess not. Let me talk to Dad."

"I am not with him now, but I am meeting with his doctor in a little while. I'll be able to ask more questions. I need to go; I'll call you after that. I promise."

As Meg and Carol ended their conversation, the nurse came out of his room, closing the door behind her.

"Nurse, excuse me, I am his wife; how is he feeling?"

The nurse sat next to her. "I just finished making up his bed, and he's awake; why don't you go in to see him, now that the parade is over?"

The nurse shocked Meg by her comment. Meg said to herself, No way! Fear to be alone with her own husband kept her in her seat. Meg had to find a way to be part of the picture again in his life. When Meg found him, she'd thought that her problems were solved—in fact, they were just beginning. In a million years, she'd never expected to be faced with this. But he was alive, and as long as he was, there was hope.

At 3:30 p.m., Meg walked to the clinic next door to meet Mariana and the doctor. No others waited. At 3:55 p.m., she could hear the quick close clip-clop, clip-clop, clip-clop of Mariana's little pointy high-heeled shoes on the floor. She had changed clothes and dressed up like a night out on the town, while Meg stood there in the same T-shirt, shorts, and sneakers. It left them five minutes to talk before their appointment with Dr. Singh, and Meg wondered if that was her plan.

Mariana took charge, reciting to Meg like she'd practiced it. "We saw Tomas and Chandon," she corrected herself, "Bitti, in the water in the dark, and we, well, my crew snagged them out and brought them aboard. We had already been cruising for a while, and without our log, I can't be sure of the date. It was about two weeks ago that we found them."

"When did you realize he didn't remember?" Meg spoke Spanish well enough to communicate this with her. And Mariana understood her.

"Immediately," Mariana quickly responded. "He didn't know his name or what had happened to him. He didn't even recognize the little dog. Then he told us his name was Tomas. My captain, he didn't hear on the radio of any searches, and we were heading east to meet my friend in Punta Cana, so we took him on. He ended up being an excellent cook. We've actually had a great time together."

"Together?" Meg's psyche didn't need to comprehend that. Meg had more to say on that subject, but Dr. Singh walked up to them.

"Come to my office, and we can talk." Meg wanted to tell her to take a hike, but good manners and good judgment said no, not yet. The doctor continued. "Tomas's condition is good, no infection. He can leave in the morning, providing his progress continues. But it sounds like he has bigger problems than the gunshot wound. If you're traveling to Sint Maarten, there is a good medical facility there. It's not pretty but the staff all have returned and it is up and running. I will prescribe additional antibiotics in case any issues arise. But also I will give you the name of a doctor you can contact. Based on what I understand, he wants to travel?"

Meg said, "Doctor, I know you didn't see my husband when they rescued him. He got thrown from the flybridge of our boat, was adrift a long time, sunburned and dehydrated. After they brought him aboard, they found out that he suffered from amnesia. I have just seen him for the first time today. He doesn't recognize me. How long can I expect this to last?"

Dr. Singh stood thinking of the best recommendation to give Meg. This time his black eyes spoke directly to Meg, but Mariana had her nose right in there. She was still clinging to Tomas.

"He probably just needs time. He could wake up tomorrow with full recall, or it could go on. It is my experience, and I am not a neurologist, that the more pleasing the care and the surroundings, and more familiar the people and things, the quicker the recovery. Maybe he might want to consider an MRI in case of a head injury."

"Ok, can you order this today? What if I just take him home?" Meg asked.

"You could do that legally, but mentally, your results might not be what you want. And having no memory, Tomas might refuse to go. I'll be glad to talk to you more; we don't have a permanent neurologist on staff here, though." He gave her his business card. "Call my office; I can get you the name of a doctor in San Juan if you are interested. I think that would be your best bet."

"This might sound odd. He is my husband, but I am afraid. Would you consider meeting with him and me and talking about his memory loss before he leaves the hospital tomorrow?"

"I can do that. But it will have to be first thing in the morning, maybe seven?"

"Yes, ok. Thank you so much, Doctor." Relief filled Meg's head. "Well, it's a beginning."

They left his office; Mariana headed out for a late lunch, and Meg went next door to the hospital. She went to Tomas's room, and when she saw the staff, they acknowledged her presence in the hallway. Through the narrow window in the door of his hospital room, Meg watched him sleeping. She went in, putting Bitti inside on the plastic chair by the door. It tortured Meg's soul. Emptiness filled her gut, and for the first time in her life, she grasped the meaning of what it felt like to have a broken heart. Yet standing by his bed, when she touched him, all her agony went away. God, she loved him. Right there at that moment, Meg accepted that her journey searching for him hadn't come to an end. Meg had found Tom Trumbo's body, but now she had to touch his mind.

Meg went online and read that there were different types of amnesia. Tom's amnesia was referred to as retrograde. *Retro* meant "before." A memory loss that began on a specific date or as a result of an incident and could go back for decades or just a few weeks or months. Interestingly, with this type of amnesia, his personality, intelligence, ability to speak, and social skills were not affected at all. How far in the past his memory loss went, Meg couldn't know. But if he ever desired to recall his past, only Meg could take him there. The only one present who knew the real Tom. That fact alone should have made him want to keep her. A plan began to form in her mind, but she needed more advice.

All her life, her husband had advised her. He called all the shots. If Tom wouldn't cooperate, she needed to find a way to peel back the new memories being made and expose the past to him in a pleasing way. The time had come for Meg, not him, to be the one making the decisions and calling the shots.

Meg knew her job.

First of all, she needed to stick close to Tom and reinvent their relationship.

Second, she needed to do research about recovering amnesiacs and names of doctors in the field in the United States that she may be able to contact for advice. Meg had a relative, a doctor, in Chicago she could call for a referral.

Third, if he was insistent on continuing on *Moet*, she needed to go with him. Outside of his room, in the hall, the nurses came in and out of rooms chattering. Then it hit her.

Meg had studied nursing in her early life. She had gone to nursing school before they married. Meg hadn't kept up with her license, but she could perform emergency lifesaving procedures, give an injection, and be an asset aboard in critical situations. She also excelled at handling lines, and she could drive the boat in an emergency. Meg decided to prepare a résumé to present to Mariana the next day. She needed to make known her authority and ability to act to take Tom home if she had to do it. If Mariana thought she had dibs on Tom, Meg had no problem standing with her, toe to toe, bosom to bosom, to reclaim her man.

The day left her time enough to search out a place she could use a laptop and a printer. She needed a few more pieces of clothing, shoes, personal items, and a larger backpack in which to carry them and now Bitti. Searching on her phone, she found a few of the familiar places where she shopped at home and way more stores that had been there ten years ago. In Saint Thomas, people spoke English, although as you traveled the islands, you needed to get used to the lingo. A man walking by Meg on the street and smiling at her amorously would be referred to as giving her the "sweet eye," and there were many other phrases a visitor would need to learn to understand the islanders.

The walk to the Office Depot store took her three miles from the harbor. South of the tourist shops, and in the same area, a Kmart and other stores frequented by residents lined the streets. On her way, she passed touristy stores open with new storefronts and remodeled interiors to attract buyers. She could see behind them in the alleys that many were still in disrepair from the water and wind damage. The vendors stood out front calling her in, offering the best deals "in all of Charlotte Amalie." In fact, they added, "in all of the Virgin Islands." There were thin five-dollar T-shirts and cheap rum, exotic pipes, and voodoo paraphernalia. Meg had a hard time ignoring them and found it necessary to say, "No, thank you, not today," at each shop she passed by. Meg wanted to acknowledge their desire to make a sale. The vendors were persistent, sometimes annoying, but only that commitment could keep people living in a climate where year after year, hurricanes threatened to wipe out their lives.

Last year thirty-two hundred inhabitants had fled the islands for the United States, although the majority still remained. Just as she'd found with Rose at the airport spa in San Juan, whether it be family, job, age, or love of country, they stayed, and Meg didn't understand their fervor to persevere.

Once at the Office Depot, she began by using one of their computers and created and printed her résumé, which she would give Mariana and her captain on *Moet* the following day. Afterward, she negotiated a good deal on a Dell laptop, paper, and a couple of thumb drives.

At the Kmart, Meg bought a pair of jeans, two blouses, one summer dress, and sexy lacy underwear in a few different colors—including black—plus two pairs of shoes. One pair of shoes were white flip-flops, the second brown leather sandals with a small heel. Tom said that heels always made her legs slender and sexy.

While Meg prepared her résumé at Office Depot, Mariana and Antonio checked in with Tomas to talk about leaving. Antonio had replaced the engine part. They wanted to depart for Sint Maarten that night and suggested that he fly and meet them in a few days. The weather forecast had changed, and they wanted to go now. Mariana still hoped to make Saint Barts by the weekend for the festival of Bastille Day, where she hoped she would see her daughter.

"No," Tomas said, "I can go with you. I am feeling fine. I can change the dressing on my arm myself. And while I may not be 100 percent, I can still do things aboard."

"With it just being Angeli and me, I could use an extra body, whatever shape it's in," Antonio added.

"Well, what about Meghan?" This time Tom Trumbo spoke. "She seemed eager to go along, and she's very capable on a boat."

Mariana's jaw dropped. She had never even gotten that feeling. What had changed with this man in the bed in a few hours? And he now said Meghan was capable on a boat? This morning, he barely knew her name and couldn't look her in the eye.

"Tomas, if you feel you are ready to go with us tonight, I'll call her," Antonio volunteered.

"No, Antonio, I'll call her," Mariana corrected him. "You help Tomas get his stuff together so he can get released, and I'll go to the boat and wait and let Angeli know what's going on. What time do we need to leave, Antonio?"

"Six," Antonio said. "We need to leave by six o'clock. Still plenty of daylight. But we have a lot to do and not a lot of time."

Meg walked all the way along the busy roadway going up the hill and stopped at the hospital. At 5:45 p.m., the little twinkling landscape lights were already lit as she walked through the pink-flowered trellises that surrounded the shaded pathway. A few cats were lying in wait watching in the lighted areas to catch lazy lizards for dinner. One had a den of newborns hiding in an overturned wooden barrel where flowers used to grow. Meg could see their tiny eyes staring out, waiting for Mama to return with dinner.

In Meg's walk down the hall to the hospital room, the overhead lights were dimmed, with small night-lights near the floor at intervals for guidance. No light shone from her husband's room. Meg found it odd for the time of day. She had planned to try to talk with him before heading back to her hotel. She opened the door. Just an empty room with the bed all made up. She hurried to the nurse's station, but no one on that shift had any details about him. Meg ran out of the hospital doors and along the pathway two blocks to the harbor front. The slip was empty, and *Moet* was gone.

Humiliation and betrayal did a double whammy on Meg and she was disheartened about the turn of events. No, Meg was pissed! After all she'd been through, she'd found him, and he'd gone.

Maybe she'd just pack her stuff and her dog and go home. Screw him!

That thinking didn't last long. Meg knew *Moet*'s float plan and was now experienced at playing their cat and mouse game. Meg ran frantically along the harbor to her hotel, gathered what little she had there, checked out, and got a taxi to the airport. She didn't have time to reminisce at the beach when the cabby drove by it. Meg moved at full speed. Her goal: to be in Sint Maarten waiting at the dock when *Moet* arrived.

The airport had one short runway on the edge of an island. There were over sunned families with their over-the-limit carry-on bags, still dressed in bathing suits and cover-ups. Meg checked the screen for the departure flights to Sint Maarten into the Juliana airport. Flights left at seven thirty every evening. She waited at the ticket counter that serviced multiple carriers. She stuffed Bitti into the screened zippered area of the backpack. When Meg bought it that day, she hadn't seen the "pet friendly" tag on the zipper. With it zippered, you could barely see the eight pounds of fluff and the little black eyes and nose peeking out at you. When it came to be her turn at the counter, the casually dressed attendant smiled at her with great big beautiful bright-white teeth. Her eyes were wide and large, and she had long eyelash extensions that fluttered when she spoke.

"How can I help you today, lady?" she asked respectfully.

Meg spoke quickly, still catching her breath. "I need to go to Sint Maarten tonight. I see that you have a flight leaving; I'd like to buy a ticket."

The gal began to access the schedule and flight. She typed so fast, and so long, it went on and on, and when Meg expected her to come forth with an answer, she typed in more. Meg had to work on her patience; it was failing her.

"Yes, there is a flight. But it's completely booked." She saw the disappointment on Meg's face. She also saw Bitti staring out the backpack over Meg's shoulder, and she smiled. "I can get you on tomorrow, same time; will it just be the two of you?" She smiled again, pretending not to notice the dog.

"I must go tonight."

"There are no guarantees, but if you go over to gate two and wait, there may be a no-show at the last minute. Take this and go to the ticket counter there. In the meantime, I can put you on for tomorrow."

"I really have to go tonight; any chance of a private charter?"

The attendant pointed to a flyer on her counter: "Sunshine Airways. We Shine for You."

Meg followed her instructions. Gate two, across from gate one, next to the line she had just waited in. No departure time or boarding time, just a sign that said "Delayed." The plane still hadn't arrived from Nanny Cay, Tortola.

At six forty-five, a few people arrived, milling around, unhappy about the delay. One said that he had taken this flight many times, and it was always delayed. He didn't like these small planes and landing at the Juliana airport at night. If she didn't know the name of the airport, she wouldn't ever have understood his lingo. But she knew about Juliana from their own trips. A free tourist attraction. The plane's scary approach to the airport brought the plane so close to Maho Beach, it kicked up the sand in the beachgoers' eyes. They lined up by the fence to watch KLM's jumbos roar in.

While she waited, Meg called the number on the flyer. The man sitting next to her answered his phone.

"Sunshine Air; we shine for you. This is Cal."

Meg turned her head to her right and stared straight into the eyes of Sunshine Air's one and only pilot, Cal. Owner and operator.

"Well, I guess you're not flying today." She smiled.

"You wanna go? I'll take you."

"Aren't you going on this plane?" Meg asked.

"Noooooo. I be waiting on my boy; his mama lives in Nanny Cay, and we share him, every other week, you know, in the summer when school's out. But if you want to go, I can take you. It must be right away, 'cause I don't fly at night."

"How much will you charge me? I am only going one way."

"I only go round trip, twelve hundred, cash, whether you return with me or not; plus, I need to stay over, 'cause I don't fly at night."

The gal with the big bushy eyelashes at the ticket counter lackadaisically moved over to gate two and announced that the plane had arrived from Nanny Cay, and after a quick cleanup, they would be boarding for Sint Maarten. Cal's boy came running in through the door from the stairs up from the tarmac. Unlike his father, he was a light-skinned islander. Big almond-shaped eyes and curly light-brown hair and a smooth complexion dominated his features. Cal stood up and waved to catch his attention, and when he came over, he grasped his father's leg.

Cal was happy to see his son, but he focused on Meg, his prospective customer, when she said, "I hoped to get on this flight, but it's booked. I am waiting to see if there are any cancellations."

"I will wait with you; we'll know soon enough."

They heard an announcement about another delay due to a refueling problem. Nothing serious but enough to move the departure of the flight into the night.

Cal said, "Now is the time, lady, if you want to go. There'll be a break in the regular air traffic for me to use the runway."

No time for indecision, and Meg agreed to take Cal up on his offer. She hit an ATM, and they walked through an exit door and out to Cal's plane. A single-engine and, she imagined, maintained adequately to fly. Would he take his boy on it for twelve hundred dollars, if it were not? Meg asked herself.

The plane was bright yellow, with a sun on the body that made it stand out on the runway. Once on board, Meg got comfortable with Bitti. There were the four of them—Cal, Meg, Bitti, and Cal's son, Jorell. The propellers were turning. Cal confirmed with the tower, and before long, they taxied and made a quick takeoff. Meg said goodbye to Charlotte Amalie. Sunset hadn't happened yet, but the colors in the sky said it wasn't far behind. In all of the rushing, Meg realized, "Darn! I forgot to look for my ring."

The flight would take fifty minutes, depending on the order of landing. Cal would radio the Juliana airport for clearance. It would be a five-and-a-half-hour trip for the motor yacht *Moet* traveling at eighteen knots, half of which would be in darkness. Cal and his boy sat in the front of the four-seat Cessna 172, and Meg and Bitti were in the rear. Once in the air, Jorell, Cal's son, had completely turned in his seat and chattered to Meg. He wanted to get in the back seats with her and Bitti. Bitti was a friendly dog, but fast-talking, rambunctious little boys made her tremble. She liked to be in control of the situation and who petted who.

Jorell squeezed in between the aisle to the back, and Bitti moved to Meg's lap. Before long, even though Meg didn't appreciate it, she and Jorell were singing songs Jorell had learned that year in school. He especially liked the "Florida Alphabet Song," and they sang it over and over until Meg knew all the words by heart. He talked about how his parents had named him after Superman's father and how he dreamed he would fly like his dad when he grew up. Cal threw in a hearty deep laugh at his son's big ambition.

"How did you fare during the hurricane? I heard Nanny Cay was just devastated," Meg said to Cal.

"Yes, as were we here. But the worst was Sint Maarten. You will see, still a long way to go; the airport closed there a long time and the bridges too."

"I was there about ten years ago, my husband and I on our boat. I remember the airport and watching those big planes come in."

"They stopped that in 2016. That's why I won't do it at night."

"What about the bridge into Simpson Bay?" she asked.

"Oh, it's open now, but the opening's still reduced, you see, because of repairs going on."

Meg had checked on her phone to get the inbound bridge openings that *Moet* could take advantage of and found the last to be three in the afternoon. The next opportunity would be at 5:00 a.m. and would mean spending the night at anchorage in the bay. Could there also be a chance that they would skip coming into Simpson Bay and continue on the next morning to Saint Barths?

CHAPTER SEVENTEEN

Dawning

After Mariana, Antonio, and Tomas agreed on the departure time, they went their separate ways. Mariana sent Angeli out with a small list of galley supplies they needed for the trip. Antonio installed a security alarm in the boat, and Tomas got his things together and made arrangements to settle his account at the hospital.

Angeli liked being called upon by Mariana. Getting the job aboard *Moet* had been a godsend. So far, neither German nor Mariana had figured it out. When Antonio had emailed her and said that there may be an opportunity for her on *Moet*, she'd taken the cheapest flight she could get, even though it meant leaving at two in the morning. It made it impossible for her to say goodbye to her family. She took fifty dollars from her cousin's birthday money and left a note. Angeli swore to herself she would pay it back. It was her only chance, and if she didn't go soon, everyone would know that beneath her white uniform, a lovely young woman hid a pregnancy in the first trimester. Angeli answered his email, and before he could tell her no, she made her plans. The whole time, Angeli prayed with her turquoise knotted rosary that when she arrived, Antonio would not be annoyed, and she would get the job.

Angeli took the job on *Moet*. There were things they didn't know about her. If they had read her résumé, they would have learned that she could cut, style, and color hair, plus do nails and pedicures and that she did fantastic foot and leg massages, and sang and played the guitar. The seventeen-year-old Angeli had many talents.

Mariana never called Meg. Tomas stood waiting for Meg on the dock. Meg, the woman on the coast guard flyer that he had in his pocket, and even though his feelings for her were uncertain, something in him said he needed to stay. Here was an example of the man Meg loved. While he didn't remember their relationship, he stirred to do right by her. So, when *Moet* pulled away from the dock in Charlotte Amalie, he stood on the dock, waving. On *Moet*'s deck, the crew, Antonio, Mariana, and Angeli waved good-bye.

Hours before dark, seas were minimal, and the engines were running well. Angeli offered to prepare a meal, another talent she had that qualified her to work aboard a large yacht. When Mariana sent her out, she had taken the liberty of buying the ingredients to make *sancocho*, a popular Panamanian recipe. The chicken, garlic, yucca root, plantains, and cilantro were easy to find. Once underway, she began marinating the chicken and making the broth for the evening's dinner. Angeli sang a song cheerfully while she worked.

Meg had traveled a long way, searching. But now the tables were turned. Tomas didn't know where to find Meg. He had no cell number or knowledge of where she stayed. The only connection to her might be with Dr. Singh. Once *Moet* left the dock, he walked up to the marina office and into the crew hospitality center. It too had been remodeled since last year's storm. The floors had been replaced with hardwood flooring. They'd added new navy and red sofas with nautical lamps. On the walls were paintings by local artists of the boating life. Tomas used the crew computer and googled Dr. Singh's website. Then he called the phone number and left a message.

"Dr. Singh, this is Tomas Ramirez. You attended me at the hospital yesterday. I checked out of the hospital and am trying to get the cell number of my wife, Meg. Maybe she left it with you? Please, call me or leave the information. Thank you."

When Tom said the words "my wife, Meg" in his message to Dr. Singh, it came out of his mouth so naturally. He didn't dwell on it, but things were beginning to fall into place in his mind like bullets in the chamber of a gun.

Tomas planned to follow up with Dr. Singh's office first thing in the morning, find Meg, and then fly to Sint Maarten to meet up with *Moet*. He found a small harborside hotel. They had one room, just vacated, and he took it. Tomas needed time to relax after the time of being up on his feet. He wanted to close the curtains and get into bed, but his stomach was empty.

A lively restaurant next door that served local Caribbean food delivered to his hotel. They had fresh-made spicy ceviche with crusty baked bread for dipping. He ordered it and two bottles of beer in a bucket with ice. He and Meg had often shared it. More memories crept in his head.

After his meal, he went out onto the small balcony and sat watching the scenes in the harbor. He took in a familiar fragrance. A yellow-and-white frangipani tree flowered there. A favorite of his and Meg's. He used to call them "French panties," and she used to laugh at him. Something was happening to Tomas Ramirez.

Below him, on the sidewalk, a couple walked a gray-and-white dog that had no tail and waddled like a bear. The sidewalk led to a small grassy area that led to a sandy beach. They rolled up their pants legs and waded in as far as they could go, urging the dog to go with them. They screamed and laughed as the dog plowed like a clown into the water and soaked them. Tomas smiled and wished he could go and join in. She threw a tennis ball on the beach, and the dog ran with it till he collapsed in the shallow water. The dog, with his massive tongue hanging out the side of his mouth, reminded Tom Trumbo of a picture from his past. Tom recognized him to be a bobtail. And he knew he'd had at least one in his life.

Tom Trumbo went inside but left the door to the patio open. The couple with the dog moved on, and it became quiet again. He pulled the drapes away from the frame of the window to better the view of the water from his bed. When he did that, he saw a sparkly reflection on the floor at the edge of the brown sisal carpet. At a closer assessment, he saw a silver-and-gold band with four small diamond chips. A unique piece, familiar to him, and he knew the owner would miss it. He'd drop it by the desk in the morning.

Tom Trumbo rose early the following morning. He checked his phone for messages, and there were none. He might need to stay another night. At the front desk, while he extended his stay, he put the ring that he'd found on the counter. The clerk, a hefty woman with short, fat fingers, admired it. She held the ring on the tip of her pinky as she examined it.

"This belongs to a little gal. She'll be missing this."

The proprietor appeared from the back room and chimed in. "Maybe it belongs to the little lady here yesterday; I have a contact number, and you can give her a call," he said to the clerk. The two of them made a little more small talk, and then the proprietor came out with an envelope. He dropped the ring inside and wrote down a phone number, and he set it in front of the clerk and near enough to Tom for him to see: 305-678-9100.

The Florida area code and the chronological order of the numbers caught his eye. The clerk confirmed the room for another night if he wanted it, and from there, Tom went out to get breakfast and then over to the clinic to see Dr. Singh's nurse.

CHAPTER EIGHTEEN

Hello, Meg

Cal called Jorell to return to his seat and buckle up, and Meg strapped Bitti into her seat through her harness. He radioed to the tower at Juliana. As they came closer to the island, the dark colors from the deeper water disappeared, and the turquoise of the sandy shallows and browns from the reef were beneath them. They were so low that Meg could see the water splashing up above the rocks.

"This is the best part," squealed Jorell.

"This is the worst part," cried Meg.

At the same time Cal decreased the speed, he encountered turbulence, and the plane seemed to drop out of the sky like a rock. Meg's lunch came up in her throat, and she let out a squeal.

The three of them laughed out loud. The plane flew over the beach and then skipped along the runway one tire and then the next, and in a short time, it came to an abrupt stop. He taxied to an area away from the hangars where small commuter planes like his lined up. Once there, he turned the engine off. Cal got out and helped Meg climb out with the dog.

"Where do you need to go? I'll call you a taxi; I know people here who can be trusted."

"Well, it's getting dark now, but I won't be able to sleep tonight unless I go to the yacht club on Simpson Bay first. Is there a hotel near there that would be a decent place to stay?"

"My friend Mike, he can take all of us, and you can choose. He knows what's open now." Meg agreed.

Once inside the customs and immigration area, still being housed in a tent, she pulled out her passport, and Tom's fell out of her bag and on the floor. When she picked it up, it opened to the page with his photo. Five years old now, but the image looked the same and not much different than when she'd seen him yesterday at the hospital. And the name he'd signed wasn't Tomas Ramirez.

Presenting Bitti's paperwork, she noted the date of her vet exam in Key West before they left. Also, she had the courtesy clearance from US Customs for Isla Mujeres, Mexico, that they never used. She'd lost track of how long it had been since she lost Tom and Bitti. It seemed longer to her than reality. That made her hold Bitti tightly. No one cared about Bitti in the immigration office, where she came from, or any papers that Meg might have for her.

After customs, they waited outside by the curb for their ride. After about ten minutes, Meg could see an old but well-kept white limousine driving toward them with a sign on the door reading Taximan Mike. Cal called out to him with words that Meg couldn't catch up with and Mike responded, and they laughed. That island lingo again that rolled off their tongues so smoothly. He used the car for weddings as well. It had a bar and little lights strung along the lining of the roof. Cal got in the front seat with Mike, and he opened the tinted privacy window between the driver and the ride. Jorell sat in the passenger seats with Meg and Bitti. Jorell opened every ashtray and compartment. He pulled out something red and lacey from one compartment and then quickly stuffed it in once he realized he had a woman's underwear. Next to champagne glasses, he found a package of condoms. He looked at them bug eyed and then peeked over at Meg to see if she saw him. Meg didn't know if he understood, but after that, he slid back in the deep black leather seat and remained silent.

From the airport, they headed to Simpson Harbor, where the marinas and hotel rooms were located. Not far on Airport Road but too far to walk in the dark. She could see as they passed by that the beaches were filled with chairs, but the lolos, normally bars and trinket shops had no merchandise and were now falling down shacks. The sand that washed ashore from the storm piled up in berms, and the bulldozers sat silent for the night. The palm trees were hurricaned with little sprouts of palms sticking up, like fingers pointing to the sky. It wouldn't take a long time for their fronds to be waving again in the breeze, adding to the romance of the island like before. When they turned into the street that led into Simpson Harbor, the security gatehouse said *Closed*, and the gatehouse was empty. Cal got out of the car and lifted the gate, and Mike drove under it. Most of the marinas in the harbor were closed for business. A fair amount of sunken sailboats sat in the water, and others sat dry-docked on land. You could see their masts protruding up from the water like building cranes. Meg wouldn't want to bring *Tori's Seacret* in there with all that mess. A few large vacant boats sat at the yacht club, but no *Moet*. Meg could only assume Moet waited outside the drawbridge, anchored and waiting to enter at the 5:00 a.m. opening.

Taximan Mike pulled up to a marina hotel. The new sign lay on the ground next to the entrance waiting to be hung. Cal got out and went inside with Meg while Mike waited. Two young men hung out in the lobby. The bartender washed glasses while his only customer, a bald man, sat at the bar. A large gaudy gold anchor hung at his neck. He held a glass of whiskey and rubbernecked Meg, his eyes loitering on her chest. Meg glanced at her two top buttons that were pulled open from the weight of her backpack. She pulled it together. Meg made an about turn, and on her way out, the men in the lobby said the front desk clerk had left for dinner.

"If you don't have a reservation, she may not return at all. There's no business here."

Cal's face questioned Meg, and she shook her head. He walked out to the car and leaned in to talk to Mike.

After a few minutes, Cal came in to meet Meg in the doorway on her way out.

"Mike says his lady is cooking tonight. She always makes plenty, and you're welcome to spend the night. Jorell and I are going too. You will be safe there with us, no worries. We'll eat, have beers, and listen to island music. Jorell will be happy if you come, and the dog is welcome too."

There she found herself again at the mercy of strangers. So unlike her to allow herself to be in situations like that. She had no choice. But Mike's offer was more good news she'd heard all day, and she trusted Cal. With some people, you just know.

Meg hopped into the limo, and Mike drove to the French side of the island. During the ride, random streetlights lit the hilly road. At the top of one high hill, with a view of French Saint Martin, it lit up enough to reveal cranes that were in the process of repairing resorts by the water. Coming over another hill, Meg saw a collage of blue plastic tarps in the valley. These were local homes still waiting for roofs. Tarps also covered windows that were blown out from the wind. At the end of the streets, there were mountains of debris. There were appliances and cars and mattresses and everything else destroyed in the flooding of the residences.

While he drove, Mike and Cal chatted about how the recovery had sped up after Macron visited from France. The people had a general distrust with the local government. Many of the families were still split up, as most of the women with small children had evacuated to Aruba and had not returned. The men who now had no jobs stayed behind to help in the rebuilding projects funded by local wealthy business owners till monetary aid started rolling in. He counted himself as lucky to find his limo spared. People needed transportation, and once gas stations were open, he kept his business going. He admitted though that for several weeks immediately after the storm, he'd driven many people many places for a buck or two, and once the gas became unavailable, he'd rented it out to an elderly couple with no place to sleep.

Shortly, they were driving over a small mountain in the center of the island closer to Orient Beach on the French side of the island. Vacant property extended a long way and ran along the water. He pulled in the drive of a very substantial stilt-style home freshly painted cornflower blue with pink trim. It had a porch that led to a breezeway that connected to another separate smaller dwelling at the rear of the property. That was where Mike's lady friend Lizbeth lived. Both homes had a generous view of the water. Lizbeth took care of the larger house when her employers were at home in Europe. She kept it maintained and prepared the home for them when they arrived each year for the season. The owner's home had four bedroom suites, a living room, a dining room, and a chef's kitchen. The living room and dining room opened up to the cool breezes coming off the water. Although the home hadn't flooded from rising water, the wind had taken a toll on the roof, which in turn had caused water damage from the days of rain that followed. Most of the repairs were complete.

Meg followed Cal, Mike, and Jorell onto the porch past the entry to the main house and then behind to Lizbeth's cottage. When they walked in, Lizbeth was laboring over the stove. Meg saw a tiny woman working over the cooktop, and she surprised Meg when she turned to greet them. Lizbeth, like Rose from San Juan, was Vietnamese but was born in the Virgin Islands. She spoke perfect English. A big white apron covered a big denim shirt and narrow-legged jeans. Standing next to Mike, her thigh was half the size of his. Her straight-cut black bangs sat squarely on her face and from there hung to her shoulders. The smells from her kitchen said French food. Lizbeth simmered a smooth dark sauce for a roast rack of lamb finishing in the oven. She was not only the caretaker of the estate but also its cook. Meg could see why Mike fancied this woman.

Lizbeth's house had two bedrooms. Cal and Jorell would take the second bedroom, and Lizbeth took Meg up to the main house.

"This is my favorite bedroom, the owner's deceased mother's suite. I spent time with her as she struggled in the end. The view is the best one on the property. Make yourself at home; everything's clean, and there are fresh towels that I put in the bath. Dinner is still an hour away; I never know with Mike's business."

"Thank you so much, Lizbeth. I could use a shower and a few minutes to relax. It's been a crazy day."

Meg got out one of her new Kmart Jacqueline Smith blouses and hung it up by the window and cracked it open a little to let humidity penetrate it. She hopped in the shower and let the hot water and steam pour around her. She closed her eyes to relax. Tom said that he had done his best thinking in the shower, but she didn't think about tomorrow. Afterward, Meg sat wrapped in her towel on a cushy chair on the patio in the dark and listened to the waves crashing up on the beach. After dinner, she could walk it and reminisce about the times that she and Tom had spent there. Meg could hear music from an accordion playing sweet sounds over at Lizbeth's, so she dressed and went over.

Mike could make his accordion weep like a guitar. He played one George Harrison song and one John Lennon. Jorell knew those lyrics, and Mike played an encore. Everyone clapped, including Lizbeth, who stood at the door, calling them to come to the table. A table large enough to seat eight people, it gave her the room to put all the food out and to serve it family-style.

Lamb was a common commodity in all the islands of the West Indies. There were sheep grazing everywhere. She placed two plates of lamb chops on the table along with lamb bones that she used to make her sauce. Mike chewed on the lamb bones smothered in some extra brown sauce, and he liked them more than the meat on the chops. The potatoes were small and browned and tasted like the grease from the roasting pan. Lizbeth boiled carrots and whipped them up with heavy cream until the carrots stood up in peaks. The carrots added a third color to the plate and made the meal complete.

Once they ate their dinner, Meg collected all the dishes and began cleaning them and started to fill the dishwasher. Lizbeth came in to object, but Meg sent her out to the porch to visit with Mike and Cal. Meg could see them from the kitchen. Mike lit a couple of Cuban cigars that Cal had brought along, and Mike passed one over to Lizbeth for a turn. Jorell stayed in the kitchen with Meg and Bitti, drying and stacking the pots and pans as Meg passed him the clean ones. Jorell wanted to finish and get out on the porch to hear Mike's stories of the hurricane recovery and maybe play a game of crazy eights. But Cal chased him into bed. He kissed everyone good night, including Bitti, and went to his room with an upside-down mouth.

Meg thanked both Mike and Lizbeth for their hospitality and delicious dinner. Meg let a big yawn slip out and excused herself. A suggestive response made Cal follow suit. Lizbeth handed Meg a snifter, and in it, she poured a generous amount of island port.

"This will help you sleep."

"Thank you again. Good night." If ever there was a time that a payment or tip was due by Meg, this was it. But now, Meg knew the difference and did not worry. Sometimes, people just want to do good for no gain. These are the unforgettable people you meet in your life. Lizbeth would be one.

Meg walked through the breezeway to the main house, grabbed an old quilt from the chair, and walked the wooden stairs to the path that led to the water with her glass of port. Seagrasses along the way had already grown tall over Meg's head. Bitti shadowed close. She draped the quilt around her shoulders and tried to sit cross-legged, but that no longer worked for her, so she lay on the sand. After one sip, Meg realized that the port was no port at all but high-quality woody cognac. She cupped the glass to warm the contents. Meg wished Tom were with her to enjoy the night and the company and the excellent food. He would have been a good guest at Lizbeth's table. And now this. These were the things they would do. Tom would give his evaluation of the cognac in her hand now. That night she made the decision of when it became ready to drink, and then she sipped it slowly. It still caught in her throat, but the potency soothed and numbed her when it went down.

The last time Tom and Meg visited, they had dinner nearby and walked that way on the beach. They'd had the big dog with them, and she'd enjoyed the best part of her day when her belly was full, and the air was cool. On that beach, the nudes would swim, and Tom wanted Meg to strip with him and swim with Matey. Meg wouldn't do it. Although they were alone, she said no. Tom became frustrated.

Meg finished the cognac, and her body felt on fire. She slipped off her blouse, shorts, and panties and lay flat out on the sand. Bitti lay on her belly next to her. Meg pulled the blanket off her naked body and gazed at the stars like she had when she lay on *Tori's Seacret*. The moment and the cognac made her nostalgic. Bitti licked her salty tears. Meg wasn't embarrassed or afraid. The last few weeks had changed her. After forty-five minutes, Meg wrapped herself, cradled Bitti, and went up to the house.

CHAPTER NINETEEN
Tom Trumbo

Tom Trumbo arrived at the doctor's office at the clinic next to the hospital. The nurse at the desk checked in people with appointments. Others lined up ahead of him at the window, and several sat in the lobby waiting to see a doctor. There were three doctors in the group—Dr. Singh and two female doctors—and a female nurse practitioner. Most of the people waiting were elderly. They were husbands and wives that had to lean on each other to get up from their chair. One carried the other spouse's paperwork and insurance cards and gave them to the nurse while the other went to find a chair. Tom found it hard to believe they were once young and vibrant. One man wore shorts and revealed legs so thin they were like two sticks. His feet had a chore as he shuffled slowly while his gym shoes seemed glued to the floor. Tom thought he may have been afflicted with Parkinson's. He had no expression on his face except maybe one that said he was done with living. The next man burst through the office door. He had a fire in his gut. He was dressed well, all smiley, kidding with the nurse, and eyeing the room for a person to talk to. About five minutes later, his wife showed up through the door, all disheveled with her short hair still in a bedhead from the night before.

"Why didn't you wait for me?" she scolded him. "I couldn't find you."

"I'm right here, dear," he wined and petted her head.

Tom pondered briefly on how they might have lived in their earlier years. He thought of things that he and his wife had done. At first, he pitied them, and then he pitied himself for his situation. Then it became his turn at the window. The nurse hadn't met him before, and when he said his name, she couldn't find any record of his treatment on her computer.

"When did you see the doctor?"

"At the hospital yesterday morning, after an accident."

"Spell your last name for me, Tom."

He began slowly and loud enough for her to hear through the window. "T-r-u-m-b-o."

"That's a fine name, but I don't have a Tom Trumbo here. I do have a Tomas Ramirez that the doctor saw at the hospital. Could that be you?"

Tom rolled his eyes. "Yes, that's me, Tom Ramirez."

Too busy of a day for this, her expression said to him.

"I left a message yesterday. I am trying to find out if my wife, Meghan Trumbo, left a phone number with the doctor."

The conversation became too weird for her, and the line behind him began building again. She asked him to sit and wait while she called the doctor when she had a moment to spare.

Tom took a seat opposite the smiley guy, who eagerly waited to talk.

"Did I hear you say your name is Trumbo? Where I came from in southern Indiana, we had a family of Trumbo's, lived on a big farm and raised horses, Tennessee Walkers. I think eight kids. You know of them?"

Tom didn't hesitate. "That would be my father's older brother, Harold, and those eight kids would be my cousins. I haven't been out there for a long time. I grew up in the city."

Just as the conversation heated up, the nurse called Tom to the window to tell him she had Meg's phone number. She had gotten it from the doctor's desk. It was a *Tori's Seacret* boat card with a picture of the sixty-one foot Viking and their names, email addresses, and phone numbers on the reverse. On it, he saw his cell number and Meg's, the same number he'd seen on the counter at the hotel that morning. A light came on in his head. Meg Trumbo had occupied the room before him. Meg Trumbo had left the ring. Lost in thought, Tom turned to leave.

"Mr. Ramirez, do you need an appointment to see Dr. Singh?"

He walked out of the office door. He left the building and called Meg's number. It rang until it found her voice mail, but he ended the call without leaving a message. Then he called Antonio.

"Hey, Tomas, buddy, where are you?"

"I am good. I am still in Saint Thomas. Where are you?"

"We are at the yacht club in Simpson Harbor. We anchored out in the bay and came in at the 5:00 a.m. bridge opening. I just washed the boat and wished you were here to help. When are you coming?"

"I am going to check out flight times. Don't know if I can come today. Have you heard from Meg? I called her. She didn't answer."

"Been working all morning, haven't seen or heard. I'll check with the boss lady—hold on." Tom waited while Antonio found Mariana and then gave him a negative.

Tom responded, "I'll call you when I have the flight details." And then they ended the call.

Tom walked to the hotel along the water; contrary to his claims, a pain radiated from his wound, more so than when he'd dressed and rushed over to Dr. Singh's office. He should have arranged for an appointment to see him before he left for Sint Maarten. He'd make that decision after he checked out the flights.

The desk at the hotel had a "Return Soon" sign written in pink marker with a smiley face on it. He called into the proprietor's office, but no one came out. He went up to his room to take his shower that he had missed that morning. At home, when they readied for the day, he called it "his shower," and she called it "hers." Words his mother and father would say, and they continued it. Tom judged that a Midwest thing.

Tom climbed the stairs after no service from the elevator. When he approached his room, he could see inside, and the generous backside of the desk clerk exiting as she vacuumed his room. He startled her in the doorway.

"Gee whiz, bud, you freaked me out. I'll be done soon." She spoke loudly over the noise and yanked the cord out of the outlet to silence it. "And I have news for you about the ring, if you wait for me to finish."

He nodded and went down to the lobby. He listened to the news on the small flat-screened TV on the wall. The Weather Channel reported that the tropics were quiet. The hurricane season officially started June 1, but no storms so far. But by mid-August, the disturbances rolled off the coast of Africa like a dealer with a deck of cards, letting the tropical waves fall where they may. Most headed west-northwest. Tropical waves turned due north, and others continued west into the West Indies, Puerto Rico, and the Dominican Republic. From there, it was a gambler's game to predict. Would it be Cuba, the Yucatán, or Central America? The Bahamas, Florida, or the Gulf or the East Coast of the United States?

Tom thought about *Tori's Seacret* for the first time. Meg had told him yesterday. Yesterday? She'd said that *Tori's Seacret* sat docked at the Hemingway Marina west of Havana. They had no insurance coverage there. She had hired a seaman to take care of her, start the engines, and arrange for cleaning while in her absence. He began to think about when he'd read Erik Larsen's book, *Great Hurricane of 1900*. It started with a mild disturbance off the Cape Verde Islands of Africa. It made the first landfall in the Dominican Republic and then skirted the coast of Cuba. Erroneously forecasted by the US weather service to turn up the East Coast of the United States, instead the hurricane moved through the Florida Straights and into the island of Galveston—forever changing the city's course in history and forcing it to surrender its golden age to Houston.

Tom and Meg had been through many hurricanes since 1998. There hadn't been a bad storm in years until they moved there. No evacuating for them. They stayed their ground and experienced every one of them. Tom set up his command center. He had car batteries in the living room to power their radio. Meg stocked food that could be cooked on the grill. She lined up gallons of water from the tap in the hallway. She filled the bathtub with more water for flushing. Another one of his adventures to experience a hurricane while others evacuated. Unfortunately, in one hurricane, they lost both cars, the first floor of their home, and irreplaceable photographs and memorabilia.

When the winds and rains of the hurricanes arrived, they came in the dark and at high tide. The Trumbo's shuttered windows shook violently twelve hours on the front side and twelve when it passed, with the storm surge following a few hours behind it. Daylight came, they watched through openings in the shutters as neighbors, boats, trash barrels, patio furniture, planters, and decorative mulch floated by their house. The surge left seaweed and sand and saltwater residue everywhere. Afterward, six-inch baby tarpon fish swam in little saltwater puddles that were created when the water came up and left them behind. Except for the palms, most everything growing on the land died.

The desk clerk stumbled out the elevator with her vacuum and buckets and entered the lobby.

"I have found the owner of the ring; she's going to describe it before I give it to her. She'll be by later."

"The lady who stayed in my room?" He knew she lied to him. The clerk responded with an "Uh huh," looked away, and went to the desk.

When Tom had bought the ring for Meg twenty years ago, it came with a choker and earrings and bracelets, each having the little studs on them. He seemed to remember that the ring cost him five hundred dollars. She wore it when they cruised, instead of her bulky wedding ring. How could she have missed it?

Tom just about remembered everything except when the wave hit and his time in the water afterward. He had flashes of Bitti when he plucked her out of the sea as she floated by him. Those tiny lungs would have never survived the waves. The hot-pink life vest that he'd objected to when Meg bought it may have saved them both.

Tom used the guest computer in the lobby and went online to check for flights to Sint Maarten. He could get one the following night. He had errands to run, but Tom's head pounded, and he felt a chill. He went up to his room and peeled off the dressing on his wound. He had to get to the doctor.

On his way out, he called to the desk clerk. "If the owner doesn't show up for the ring, I'll buy it from you. I'll be back later." He knew she'd never called Meg and probably would take a couple hundred for it. When he found Meg again, it may turn out to be a good peace offering.

A fair amount of people sat in the doctor's office lobby waiting. The same woman sat at the reception window. When Tom signed in with both names, she smiled and jokingly asked which name he was using this afternoon. She knew she had been tough on him earlier and tried to be helpful. She signed him in, and not long after, she called his name.

The cute young nurse practitioner took his temperature. She had him remove his long-sleeved *Moet* shirt, and she acted unaffected when she saw his build. Most of her patients were over seventy. Keeping it all business, she brought up the chart, reviewing with him about how the injury occurred. When she removed the dressing, she saw what Tom had seen in his room. It had become infected.

"How long has this been this way?" She shook her head. "That is why the doctor wanted you to remain in the hospital. He is here now, and I will have him come in and see you. Be patient."

"What could I have done wrong?" Tom thought.

Tom waited probably thirty minutes before Dr. Singh came. The doctor moved quickly. Tom had seen doctors like this before, who had not many words. The nurse cleaned the wound thoroughly after the doctor saw it.

"I am going to prescribe a different antibiotic for you. You need to take it faithfully every four hours until it is gone, and the dressing needs to be attended to every four hours also. I am also giving you a product to apply to the area to promote healing. You can also use that on your facial scars. You will be ok. You need to rest and keep out of the heat. Let your body heal itself."

"Thank you, Doctor. It just hit me this afternoon."

"How's your memory?" Tom didn't even know that he knew. "Your wife came to me very concerned and wanted to know how to best help you. She is a nice person."

"Last night and today, I am remembering, not just bits and pieces. I can't recall our accident when we lost our boat. I remember being frightened and worried about my wife. I remember lots of fear."

The doctor agreed, "Those memories of a tragedy may never return. The mind protects itself from remembering a trauma. And after a while, you will learn that particular time in your memory has no purpose in your life. You don't learn from it necessarily. It's like a Band-Aid on the brain. It will melt away in time." Tom liked Dr. Singh's explanation of memory loss, and Tom thanked him for going out of his way by asking and giving his personal time.

Tom went to his room and slept for most of the day. He brought in more ceviche and a beer for dinner. In the morning, Tom would hit up the desk clerk and buy the ring.

CHAPTER TWENTY

Girlfriends

W hile Antonio spent his time cleaning outside, Angeli spent hers cleaning inside. Her beautiful voice brought merriment to the yacht, and Mariana enjoyed it. She rarely sang too loud. Angeli sang "Coucouroucoucou Paloma." Mariana had heard strolling mariachis perform it in Mexico's streets. Tourists would pay the old man with a guitar and a sombrero to play the song about the cooing dove. One would pay him, then another and another. The haunting voice of the lovesick bird filled the streets. In restaurants, the tequila shots were passed, and the diners chimed in until the whole restaurant crooned. Some men even cried. A sad love song made laughable by a tuneless crowd.

God had given Angeli perfect pitch. She sang softly. Then other times, she sustained her voice a full octave above middle C. When Angeli did that, Antonio stopped in place and held his breath, waiting for her perpetual note to shatter a crystal before it disappeared into thin air. She could have been a star, but she spent her life cleaning toilets for the wealthy on a yacht in the Caribbean.

Mariana deduced that Antonio liked Angeli. He carried the baskets to the laundry room and took the heavy bags of trash to the receptacles on the docks for her. Antonio refilled her thermos with cold water, and when she rubbed her neck, he urged her to sit and take a break. In the mornings, Mariana heard her retch off the side of the boat. One evening from the upper deck, envious eyes watched them on the stern, sharing a glass of leftover red wine. One of the perks of working on *Moet*. Antonio's lady friend lived in Panama, and at the end of the cruise, when the yacht sat idle at the port, Antonio told Mariana he would return to her for a connubial visit.

Other than Hulia, Mariana had no one trustworthy in her life. Just when she'd gained ground with Tom, Meg showed up. Mariana's jealousy made her feel inadequate. It made her do and say things she regretted later. It never allowed her to find fulfillment in her life. She found herself looking over her shoulder; afraid an attractive woman might steal her man, and at the same time, Mariana wanted to do the same thing. In the endless sessions Mariana spent with her therapist, she warned Mariana. "Everyone has moments in their lives when they feel envy or jealousy. A sign that some things needed to change. To have a rewarding life, you must make it your goal to keep it under control. If you don't, you will end up ugly and alone."

At age sixty, Mariana already walked that path. She knew their marriage had ended long before. She wanted to believe that German set Max and Camilla afloat in a raft. But German had just gone along, hoping to step into Max's Gucci flip-flops when Max was gone. And her daughter had given up on her for never taking control of her life. Her own daughter loved that philandering father more than she loved Mariana. And Mariana also had known that, eventually, German would take her to her bed for her boat and her money.

She was all alone. At a time of her life when Mariana found companionship to be most important to her, loneliness moved in.

On that day, three things occurred. First, Hymie called for Mariana. Second, Meg Trumbo showed up in Sint Maarten at the dock. And third, German Veneto arrived there too. It was a complex set of circumstances that could have become more complex only if Tom Trumbo had arrived also.

Hymie's phone call reported to Mariana that German had disappeared after his release. So far, he had not kept his end of the bargain.

"Did you really expect that he would, Hymie? I didn't."

"Well, Mariana, your crew should be aware, in case he shows up."

Mariana barely listened. She discussed an issue more important to her.

"I want to purchase a new yacht. A larger one, more modern. One that can accommodate a lot of people and a big crew to accommodate them."

"What are you talking about here, Mariana? How big? How many people? How big of a crew?"

"Double the size of *Moet*. Thirty cabins and enough crew quarters for forty."

"Woooeeee, Mariana! Sounds like *The Love Boat*." You can't even deal with a crew of three without an awful lot of drama." Hymie was losing his temper. "How much do you expect to pay for a yacht like this?"

"We both know I've got it, Hymie. Make it happen."

Hymie went to the other reason for his call.

He sympathetically pled his case. "Mariana, Elena called my office again; your daughter is asking about you. When are you going to call her? She is concerned about how you are, traveling alone, and how easily someone could take advantage of you. I have to agree with her, given what just has happened in the last few weeks. You need to spend time with her. Maybe consider living at least part of the time near her. Please, will you call her?"

Excuses spilled out of her mouth, but Hymie spoke the truth.

"She has her own life, Hymie. What would I do living in Mexico City? I invited her to spend time with me in Saint Barth's for the festival, but she says she has no time." Mariana's patience faded. "Why is she calling you? Stay out of this; just do what I pay you to do."

"Mariana, did you hear what I just said? Forgive me, but you are no spring chicken anymore. It's what people at your age do. Be near family." Silence. "Mariana, do you hear me? Mariana?" Hymie asked a little too loud.

No, she didn't. She'd pushed *end call* after the "spring chicken."

At about the same time Mariana spoke with Hymie, Meg arrived at the dock. Antonio saw her walking on the pier with Bitti, and he called out to her.

"Meg. Hello!" He stopped working and jumped off to greet her. "Let me go tell Mariana you are here."

"I brought the résumé that I wrote for you, but you left before I could bring it," Meg said. "Is Tom here?"

Antonio felt bad. "No. Tom stayed behind to find you. He is coming tomorrow on a late flight. Mariana said she called you. She said you never returned her call, and we needed to go because of the weather."

His excuses made her feel better. She recovered from the humiliation and betrayal. Tom had pity for her, not love, but Meg got over that too.

Mariana came out to the gate at the boat's handrail, wearing a tunic made of blue-and-orange Acapulco silk. The V-neck revealed just the right amount of cleavage to be attractive, and it lay without a glitch on her backside over her spiffy navy leggings. In contrast, Meg stood in her baggy navy boat shorts and a wrinkled *Tori's Seacret* T-shirt.

Mariana took a deep breath and gave a long sigh. "Come on, Meg, come aboard. Get your bags; we need to talk."

"This is all I have." She raised her backpack in one fist and Bitti in the other.

"Tom is arriving late tomorrow." It was the first time Mariana had ever referred to him as Tom and not Tomas. "This will give us time to get to know each other."

For the moment, Meg felt pleased. She might have an opportunity to talk to Mariana about Tom's ordeal, to better understand how she could help him. Angeli showed Meg the way to the suite forward of Mariana's. Angeli opened the door to the cabin; she turned and quickly gave Meg a hug and left with no words.

"What does this mean?" Meg thought. "Angeli is a loving person. What did she know?"

Meg didn't know about Max or that she got the suite Mariana had shared with him. Meg had never been aboard a yacht like *Moet*. She called it a boat, but once aboard, she appreciated its luxury and elegance and why it should be called a motor yacht. As much as their *Tori's Seacret* had, *Moet* had ten, no twenty, times more.

Yellow and golds with white trim decorated the walls. Meg loved the small seating area and a window to the water when she opened the shade. On the wall to either side of the dresser, two long, narrow paintings hung in matching gold frames. Pictures of Mariana at a younger age. In both, she sat partially clothed. One was a view from the back, at her dressing table, and she glanced over her shoulder at the viewer. She sent an erotically evil smile. The artist had painted the second painting as she posed from the front. It must have been before the implants, because her breasts were small and in proportion to the rest of her body. In that work of art, Mariana's expression said loneliness. No smile. Maybe before the drugs and booze ruined her. Both canvases left a question in Meg's mind. Meg stood and wondered which represented the real Mariana. Maybe both. Maybe neither.

Meg stayed in her shorts and T-shirt. They were clean. No need to try and compete with Mariana. She added a little lipstick and brushed her hair behind her ears. In the mirror, the freckles sprayed on her nose had joined together in one big one from too much sun. She hadn't liked the patches before, and she really didn't care for them now. Now she had a brown nose. She came to the upper deck, where Mariana sat on a lounger. She sat with her view to the harbor, where the least evidence of hurricane damage existed.

Mariana acted cool. She didn't look at Meg when she spoke. "Angeli is bringing us iced tea; I would love wine, but it's too early for that. She'll bring us sandwiches too. She is serving us warm corned beef on rye."

"I love corned beef. Tom makes wonderful corned beef," Meg added.

Mariana wanted to say that Tom had made the corned beef and frozen it, but she compassionately kept it to herself. Meg woofed hers down while Mariana picked hers apart, removing the bread and kraut. Mariana started talking, and Meg sat and listened, having to periodically push her lower jaw up to close her mouth. If Mariana's statements were factual, her life would make a best seller.

Mariana rattled on about how she'd grown up in Portugal with her grandparents on their family estate. A third-generation international producer of olive oils and honey remained there. Having been educated in a private Christian girls' school, she spoke Spanish and Portuguese and more English than anyone knew. Now that her parents and grandparents were gone, just she and her daughter, Elena, were the heirs. Her husband had left her for *Moet*'s chef. He'd hoped and schemed to earn a big chunk of her wealth in the settlement.

"My husband left me because of the way that I am. I despise him for how he did it, but I understand why." This led to silence when Mariana's eyes filled with emotion. Meg waited for what came next. "I have memory loss, and I hallucinate."

Meg didn't know how to respond to her. She didn't know her well enough to console her, and did Mariana want that? Meg took a big gulp of her iced tea and wished it had been spiked to wash down the sandwich and loosen her lips. But she kept silent and listened.

Mariana continued. She confessed that there were things that happened on *Moet* that only she knew about. She didn't know if they were dreams. Meg wondered where her declaration of guilt was headed and how long it would take her to get there. Why was Mariana telling her all this? Meg wanted to grab her dog and her backpack and get the hell out of there. Meg needed to use the head, and time had come for Bitti, too, which was as good an excuse as any to take a break.

Antonio came into the galley and reported to Mariana that he thought he saw German coming out of the liquor store out on the street. Mariana didn't show concern, and it confused him. Angeli responded so fearfully when she heard that she went to her cabin and refused to come out. Thankfully, Antonio had wired up a new security camera and alarm that he'd bought in Ponce.

German sat in a clear view of *Moet* on the far end of the marina property. He had a six-pack by his side with a bag of ice on top. His eyes followed Meg and Bitti along as they meandered by him to a small grassy area. They had never met, but he recognized her from the coast guard flyer and the dog. He knew the dog. German thought. What a regrettable misfortune for him when this woman's husband entered his life.

Meg knew German as the man at the bar at the hotel last evening. The creepy one whose stare chased her back into the limo with Cal and Mike. Meg did not know him to be the captain of *Moet* or the person who had left the message for her in Punta Cana—or that he had saved Tom's life and then almost ended it. But German knew Meg, and she gave him a pain in his ass.

When Meg returned to the boat after walking Bitti, Mariana hid in her room and didn't appear again until four o'clock. When she did, she came out barefoot in loose-fitting silk animal-print pajamas that were unbuttoned too low for Meg's comfort. Mariana complained about loud music from the dock that had woken her. Angeli, cleaning crystal at the bar, looked confused. She'd heard nothing, and neither had Meg. A wall of mirrors went from floor to ceiling where small brackets made from acrylic held her expensive glassware in place. It took all day to keep them clean and sparkling. A champagne bucket affixed with museum wax was secured to the top of the bar. The high-backed swivel barstools were gold velvet with black stripe welting, and Meg anxiously waited to go up to the bar and sit on one.

Mariana read her mind. Mariana strolled over, poured from an open bottle of red, and sat crouching and scowling at herself in the mirror. When Mariana caught sight of Meg in the reflection, she acted surprised to see her. Angeli kept an eye on her, asking herself whether she should continue cleaning or leave the bar area.

"When did you arrive?" she asked Meg. Meg cautiously prepared to meet the second Mariana depicted in the painting in her cabin. "Ah, ha! I fooled you." Mariana turned from the bar and patted the barstool next to her and called Meg over.

"Come sit with me, but before you do, pick any one of those glasses for yourself," she ordered Meg. There were glasses for deep, full reds and others for lighter, more transparent wine choices. There were very large snifters for cognac and delicate crystals for the port.

Meg reached for a yellow-and-white flowered goblet, and when she did, Mariana blurted at her, "That one's my favorite."

Meg froze in place. "I'll choose another," Meg apologized.

"No, you have excellent taste. I want you to experience drinking from a piece of artwork. But we need to open an exemplary wine for that glass."

Meg became embarrassed, and she objected. But Mariana would have no part of it, and she pulled out a bottle of 1982 Chateau Mouton Rothschild from the cooler. John Houston, the noted director, had designed the label. It came with a two thousand dollar price tag. Mariana opened it and poured a little in the glass. First, Mariana swirled it and took a sip. Then she put the glass up to Meg's lips. When Meg drank from it, the rim of the glass felt so delicate—so thin she thought she might break it, or the edge could slice her lips. The Mouton drank beautifully in the yellow-and-white glass. But Meg didn't let on to Mariana that she had tasted it before.

They continued to pass it between them until Mariana chose an equally fragile crystal and poured each of them a generous share of the bottle. And after she did that, Mariana leaned over and pressed her lips on Meg's. Meg had spent her life under the control of a man but never a woman. Meg asked herself. Who does this?

Mariana exercised her method to take control. It didn't work. Meg pulled away, and the back of Meg's hand pushed Mariana away.

Meg's eyes were like saucers, shocked that she'd reacted so harshly.

"I deserved that," Mariana confessed.

Mariana moved on and began to tell the story of the history of both glasses. One came from President Fox of Mexico and another from Fidel Castro. They'd belonged to her grandfather. She didn't address the rest of them, but Meg assumed they all had a fascinating story of how she'd come to own them.

The rest of the evening, Mariana's thoughts and words bounced around. First, she talked about how she had given Meg a suite and left Tom in his crew's quarters to sleep alone. "That way, when Tom arrived aboard, he could come to you when he felt ready, and you could reunite on your own tender terms and time. You wouldn't be forced to sleep with him."

Mariana had done a lot of planning and thinking.

"More creepiness." Meg's face had a hard time hiding her disgust. It came off so impersonal. Meg had words to respond to that, but it was not worth it to her, and she just let it be.

Mariana moved to talk about her daughter, Elena—whom she now didn't know would join her in Saint Barts—and then to talk about her worries of her health and her wealth and of *Moet.*

"Now that we know each other, I feel comfortable putting a major portion of my wealth in your hands. I have already spoken to my attorney, and he is going to make it legal. I love my daughter, but we are two different women of a different time. She is being taken care of, but I would never trust her to do what I want to do."

"Why me, why us?" Meg asked. "Have you talked to Tom about this? What does he say?"

"No. I haven't. But you are here now, and when Tom comes, we'll talk more and make our plans. But I must admit to you, Meghan—do you like to be called Meghan or Meg?"

"I like to be called Meg; it's easy, and Tom calls me Meg."

"I tried to seduce him. But Meghan, in his mind, he remained loyal."

Meg became angry and wanted to slap her again. Mariana had gone too far. What does she want from us? Meg thought. But she remained silent. They had more wine and then a beef stroganoff dinner that Angeli prepared for them. As they talked more, Meg didn't see any real malice in Mariana. She saw signs of severe depression. As the night continued into dawn, Mariana laid out her plans to Meg. Mariana never gave Meg her opportunity to speak, but they sat on Mariana's boat, on her stage.

"I want to ask you," Mariana said, "do you believe in heaven and hell?"

"I don't know, Mariana. I want to. I have always thought of myself as a Christian."

"I have a hard time figuring out what the world would be like without me. Have you ever thought about that?" Mariana hesitated. "How could there be the ocean, the sky, the sun if I am not here to see it? If I die, will it cease to be? It will be the end. There must be a word for that feeling."

Mariana had just told Meg that she, Mariana, believed the world revolved around her. She thought that when she died, the world would end for everyone.

Then Mariana continued, "I have the feeling of *saudade* when I think of my homeland of Portugal." *Saa deitz*, she pronounced it so beautifully. "Do you know that feeling, Meg?" Meg did not, nor did she know the word. "It is the yearning and desire for the past, as a child, when my bare feet touched the soil of my ancestry."

Meg listened closely.

"I need to go back. Did you ever feel that yearning?"

Meg could not. Her past was so limited. She'd never felt the need to go back to Chicago and stand in her bare feet in their backyard. She and Mariana's lives were miles apart. She looked at Mariana differently, and her heart forgave her.

Meg saw Mariana as a woman who contemplated death. When Mariana and Meg left each other that early morning after that long day and night of revelation and confession, Meg knew more about Mariana than Mariana knew about her. Mariana chose her, and to Mariana, they were connected.

Meg tried not to think about Mariana's "in his mind, he remained loyal" comment. Two weeks previous, a rogue wave had capsized their boat and taken away her Tom, and that evening, she'd learned the wave was nothing in comparison to Mariana Wells.

CHAPTER TWENTY-ONE

Reunion

In Saint Thomas, Tom had the whole day to get a few things done before he had to be at the airport. He got his shower, shaved, packed up the little clothing he had, and checked out. At the hotel, he used the computer in the lobby to read news from home. He went to the *Keynoter* on the net and read about progress in rebuilding Marathon after Irma. The restaurants where they'd eaten and the stores where they'd shopped had not reopened. Tom found the number of a captain that they'd used for repairs and once for transporting the boat when they bought it.

When Tom called him, Patrick answered immediately. Patrick could do most anything around a boat. For what he couldn't do, he knew qualified people to get the other jobs done. When Patrick heard Tom's voice, he recognized him.

"Hey, bud, great to hear from you. Where are you? Heard so much bad news and then heard from your wife to come to get the boat in Havana, but then I didn't hear from her again."

"Long story; we are both fine. The boat's still in Havana. I don't know when I'll be getting there—hopefully soon. Where are you?"

"In Destin, picking up a boat and making a delivery to Charleston."

"That should keep you busy for a while," Tom said.

"Actually, I am hoping to leave tomorrow, going through the ditch and then north. Be flying home as soon as I can. Do you need help?"

"I may ask you to go to Havana and check on the boat and maybe bring her to me. Not sure yet exactly where I'll be. I should know more soon. I just wanted to touch base with you."

"Ok, have nothing going on after this, so let me know."

Tom finished the call, and he saw the hotel proprietor working at the desk, and he inquired about the ring.

"I see the ring is still here in the office safe, and the lady didn't respond to my girl's calls about it," the proprietor commented.

Tom didn't explain to the proprietor his and Meg's relationship. Tom just offered to buy the ring, hoping to bring it with him, along with a yellow-and-white frangipani tree that he might be able to buy at the Kmart outdoor nursery. They agreed on a price on the ring. Tom paid him with cash. He signed his name and address in the guest book, under Meg's, and he smiled. She had always been following him; now, for the first time in their lives, he followed Meg.

Tom arrived at the airport very early with his tree. He grabbed a hot dog and a cola. People in the terminal considered him odd as he walked with the three-foot flowering tree. Tom wrapped up its black bucket with plastic to keep the soil and water from making a mess. Meg would be proud of him for that. *I'm sorry* didn't come easy to him, and he hoped this and the ring would say it for him. Although inside, Tom suspected it would not be that easy. Not only did Tom remember more and more about himself before *Moet* found him, but Tom also knew the things he'd done after. Tom would have to deal with that. Tom wasn't one for excuses.

Sitting at gate one, he struck up a conversation with a new married couple from Omaha. They were flying to Sint Maarten and then taking a ferry to Saint Barts. She asked if he had ever been there before. She had so many intricate tattoos all over her body that he had a hard time appreciating her lovely facial features and figure or answering her question. He didn't think that people from Omaha wore tattoos. Definitely a clear indication of their difference in age. He kept trying to figure out how long it took to do all that to her body and just how far below her low-slung jeans the tattoos went. There were phrases inscribed that began with "eat," but he could only see the beginning of the next word, and he had to only imagine where that went. These were thoughts that many a man can't control, even though he tried to pull his eyes away. Jet black, straight hair combined with blood-red lipstick set off a face that never saw the sun. When he spoke to her, he kept seeing her like a snake, and it gave him the willies.

The guy was also tall and skinny, like a two-by-four—and also as white as white could be, with red spiked hair and freckles. Those were the only markings on his body. Visually they were the oddest pair, but they were pleasant and spoke intelligently about world and government affairs. When they touched one another, he could see tenderness from him and brittleness in her. He imagined their story, and he wondered what they thought about him, this old guy with a tree. In the end, he found out the guy was a neurologist, and the woman was a pulmonologist. They both studied in Arkansas. Tom thought about an idiom Meg said about a book and its cover. Once on the flight, Tom went his way, and they wished one another a good time on their vacations.

The full flight evidenced that the tourist trade had returned to the Dutch/French island. The fifty-minute trip brought them into Juliana airport in record time, although the immigration moved slowly and customs was not understanding about the tree. It cost him a sawbuck for each blooming yellow flower, although they said if he pinched them off, it would be only half. Doing so was not an option, so they taxed him two hundred dollars for a fifty-dollar tree in a bucket. The local security guard sitting at a desk along the wall smiled and said he'd gotten a good deal. Tom didn't know if that was a joke or not.

Taximan Mike waited, making pickups, and Tom got in with five others with his tree for five bucks plus a tip to take him just a couple of miles to the Simpson Bay Yacht Club. The tourists were from Iowa, dressed in cargo shorts and flip-flops, getting a good deal on rooms at the off-season price plus a hurricane special. At customs and immigration, they were buying island drinks while they waited, and each of them, except Tom, had one.

"All right," one called out. "We are ready to party."

Tom called Antonio as planned once in the limo. For the little time they'd known one another, Antonio had become a good friend to Tom. From the beginning, he'd gone the extra mile for Tom. Tom missed him.

Without Antonio and Angeli, Tom may not have survived. But more than missing Antonio, this time, Tom couldn't wait to see Meg.

"Hey, buddy, glad you called. A lot is going on here. You should know, German has been here hanging by the docks. Don't know what he's thinking. He's not supposed to be here. Mariana's in a mood. She spent the whole day and night sitting up with Meg talking."

"Maybe talk to Mariana, or maybe you should call the police. He can't be up to any good," Tom suggested.

When Tom heard that Mariana and Meg were having conversations, he wasn't concerned. He welcomed any news to make his arrival smoother. The things Tom had seen in the last days—the bobtail from the balcony, the ring, the frangipani, and Meg's signature on the guest book at the hotel—had caused things to fall in place. He had always been loyal to his wife, and now he had to deal with what he had done. Tom's heart told him to be truthful. How he'd go about it, he would need to decide.

By the time they ended the call, Taximan Mike's limo had pulled in at the end of the dock. When he dropped him, he commented to Tom, "There's a little lady with a cute little dog staying on that yacht there."

"Yeah, I know," Tom thought.

"Say hello from Mike. Tell her that Lizbeth is cooking tomorrow, if she's still in town." It didn't surprise Tom that, in such a short time, Meg had made a friend or two.

Tom walked to the yacht; after sleeping here and sleeping there, he longed to lie in his own bed. Like anyone would be after a vacation or a hospital stay. He remembered being fearful at first, realizing he had no memory or identity. He'd carried false ID and passport like a criminal. Now he relaxed in his own skin. And he yearned for the touch of Meg's.

Tom didn't see German on the dock or near *Moet*. Antonio waited for Tom at the gangplank. When Tom approached *Moet*, Antonio called out to him. "Tom." How did he know to call me Tom? Tom thought. They shook hands, and when they did, Antonio touched Tom's arm warmly. "So glad you finally are here; we have stuff to talk about, plans to make."

He and Tom had become friends, and even though Antonio's shirt said "Captain," he treated Tom like he was in charge. It may have been because of their age difference, but Antonio understood respect. Tom didn't know if he deserved it after the past few weeks, but Antonio saw a quality in him. And Tom felt the same way about Antonio.

The pieces that were missing from the picture of Tom Trumbo's past now completed the puzzle. Maybe a higher force brought it together. For the first time in his life, Tom sensed spirituality in a way he'd never imagined. You can't make this stuff up. The accident aboard *Tori's Seacret* had brought him to a place in his life he needed to be.

Moet looked good, lit from bow to stern with the lights he had replaced and restrung when he first came aboard. It was a beautiful yacht. He heard music. Tom knew the song. Bonnie Raitt, one of Meg's favorite American songwriters. From the dock, he could make out the song's words. The three girls were singing the song, "Something to Talk About." He could see the outline of the women in the dark on the upper deck dancing in a circle like three teenagers. He saw Angeli, with her little belly; Mariana, with her long flowing hair; and his wife, Meg. Pride overwhelmed him when he saw her.

Through all that had happened, Meg had grown into her own person, happy up there strutting her moves. For the short time that she and Tom had been apart, Tom had not been making the decisions and telling her what to do. Not that either of them would have chosen it, but it was an episode that had to happen between them. At times, Tom realized his responsibility for Meg's missed opportunities, her choices, and, sadly, her dreams. But after all their years together, Tom should have known well enough that she lived the life she wanted. Meg never blamed him for the life she led; she never considered it as stolen. He satisfied her, and he completed her.

Bitti raised her ears and inhaled Tom's scent, then let out a woof and hopped down the stairs to the gangway.

"Tom, stay here. I'll go up and get Meg," Antonio suggested. Tom had to face her alone without an audience. The music stopped. Angeli continued cleaning up in the galley; Antonio moved up to the pilothouse, and Mariana sat in the flybridge, where she could watch Meg as she waited at the gangplank for Tom to walk aboard.

A tough moment gripped Tom. He didn't know how to begin. He set the frangipani tree on the deck. Bitti looked at Meg and then at Tom, and when no one moved or said a word, Bitti sat next to the tree and waited. Meg spoke first. "Nice tree."

"I got it in Saint Thomas at the Kmart. I brought it on the plane, and it cost me two hundred fifty bucks in all to get it here. You notice I wrapped the bucket nicely in plastic." He spoke faster than she had ever heard him speak. They had been married thirty years, but the moment was awkward. "And I brought this too."

He held out his fist and opened it. Meg's tiny ring lay in his palm. When Meg saw it, she was awed with disappointment that she'd forgotten and left it behind. He'd remembered. How could she have left it? And where had he found it?

"I found it on the floor in my hotel room, your hotel room." And then he told her how he'd gotten it. He told her about the yellow-and-white frangipani tree growing next to the patio, and Meg remembered it, and then he told her about the bobtail outside his window. That got the words flowing between them like an open faucet. He asked her, and she told him, and she asked him, and he filled her in on everything that had occurred—except for after the wave—until he woke up on *Moet*. She told him about Jhosep and Juan, and he expressed his gratitude that they'd rescued her, treated her so well, and gotten her to Havana. She told him she had called Patrick to come and get her and the boat, and he said he had just talked to him that day. Then she told him about the two sailors who saw Bitti on her phone and then said they'd seen a dog just like her and a weather-beaten, sunburned man in Luperón.

"That's how I found out you were still alive, Tom. Oh my God, Tom, can you imagine how I felt? I could have missed hearing of you by one day. Because then, they were gone."

Meg began crying, and Tom did too. He held her there for a very long time against the bulkhead, and he pressed himself to her body, and every inch of hers touched his. His desire made his fingers spread wide on both sides of her head when he kissed her. Meg withered, and Tom kissed her again, tenderly. She led him away to the yellow-and-gold suite that Angeli had prepared for them.

Before the door closed, Bitti tucked in her tail and slipped in too. Tom and Meg fell into the cushy bed. Tom's touch unmasked feelings from Meg's younger years when he sent shivers up her spine. The time Meg had spent without him magnified her love for him now.

They found themselves naked before the paneled window in the bulkhead that offered a view to the waterline, allowing only a passing dolphin to witness their lovemaking. Tom and Meg had so much to talk about, but not then. That night they were lovers. Tomorrow they would make plans.

In the cockpit, Mariana sniveled and held her ears to block out Tom's words. Mariana grabbed a bottle of wine from the cooler and swallowed a few purple hearts. A long sleepless night was ahead of her, so she took two more.

"I have all the money in the world. No one can help me, and I cannot help myself." She stretched out on her side in her bed, and she tormented herself over her life until she fell unconscious.

German Veneto leaned against a burned-out lamp on the dock, waiting for an opportunity to make his move. Antonio had erred in not alerting security. Meg and Tom were in their cabin; Antonio and Angeli were together. That left Mariana passed out from wine and drugs. *Moet* stood at a disadvantage. German began releasing the lines where he could and cutting the others with the machete he had on his belt.

When he finished, German climbed aboard and brought in the gangplank. He crept in the shadows. In Meg's cabin, Bitti's eyes were open, and she listened for sounds like she always did. She raised her head and her ears when she heard a sound out of sorts on the boat. Bitti's nose got a whiff of trouble. She was familiar with German's smell, and she whined, instead of letting out a bark. If she did, they'd scold her. Tom and Meg didn't have an animal's natural ability to sense danger.

German's knowledge of the yacht made accessibility to its electrical systems simple. Antonio's phone signaled illegal access to the boat from the security device he had installed. German had no idea it existed. Antonio responded immediately and drew a weapon from his bedside. Angeli woke up, and Antonio muzzled Angeli's mouth and signaled a "shush" with his finger on his lips. She locked the door behind him when he left. Then, except for the emergency lighting at the base of the companionway, *Moet* went dark.

Antonio's responsibility as *Moet*'s captain was to secure *Moet* and protect Mariana. He went to the bridge and found that the boat was away from the dock. In the strong current, they drifted toward the drawbridge. Antonio lowered the anchor, and when he heard it catch, he went toward Mariana's cabin. He checked the door. He gently turned the door handle and peeked in. Mariana lay faceup, asleep. He locked the door with his key and left her secure in her cabin. Unfortunately, on the floor on the other side of the bed, German hid with his machete.

From there, Antonio went to the rear of the boat and down the rear companionway stairs to Mariana and Max's suite, where Tom and Meg were sleeping. He tapped softly and heard little woofs from inside. He waited and then did it again. Meg opened the door just a crack to find Antonio standing there. He whispered, "I am sure German is on the boat. He has tampered with the electrical system. Stay inside. Lock the door."

Tom heard Antonio at the door. He dressed and went out to find Antonio. Meg locked the door behind him. Meg paced and became impatient. She wanted to go after him, but she needed to listen. Meg slipped on a T-shirt that barely covered her new lacey panties. She sat on the edge of the bed, listening. Bitti cocked her head and listened also. Her belly spurted out another little woof that needed to come out. Meg told her no.

Tom had been gone for at least ten minutes. Meg's cabin patio doors opened to a small walkway on the port deck. The same side of the boat as Mariana's cabin. Meg slid the door open, and Bitti escaped out the door and followed the walkway toward Mariana's balcony.

"Oh. No. Bitti. Come here," Meg whispered. Meg went after her and crept along the deck barefooted, keeping low and hurrying to catch up with Bitti, who followed a scent, being true to her rat-chaser breed. She searched for German.

Antonio searched through the salon for evidence of an intruder, and Tom caught a glimpse of Antonio running with his weapon drawn. Tom shadowed him with no words and crept along cautiously. The boat began moving again. *Moet* dragged its anchor with no one at the helm. When Tom caught up, Antonio whispered to him, "I need to get to the helm. Take the gun. Keep searching."

Meg continued outside on the port side of *Moet*. A solid stainless steel, four-foot gate divided Meg's cabin's patio from Mariana's for privacy. Bitti ran under it. Meg tried to open it, but it was locked. Meg climbed around on the outside of the gate and straddled the rail. The rushing water shocked Meg, and she lost her balance and tilted back and banged her head on the hull. She ended upside down like a kid on the monkey bars. She kept her grip, and like an action character with superhuman powers, she pulled herself up and over onto the patio outside of Mariana's cabin. Meg stood ready to act.

The blinds on the patio doors of Mariana's cabin were raised about a foot from the floor, and the doors were open. The slits were open also, and a night-light lit the room, so Meg could see the scene in the room like a scene in a play. She could see Mariana lying in her bed, sound asleep, still dressed in that colorful silk tunic. Her chestnut hair lay spread around her head on the pillow with her hands folded like a Madonna in prayer. German stood over her with his machete prone to strike her chest. He sobbed. Afraid to affect the moment and cause him to act, Meg held her breath. Bitti stood at German's feet and let out a big woof for a little dog, and Meg went for it.

Like a 747 landing at Juliana airport, Meg crashed through the blinds. She pushed German, and he stumbled onto the floor away from Mariana. Meg picked up Bitti and moved away from him. German got up and lunged at her with the machete, crisscrossing it in front of her. He grazed Meg's arm as she swirled away, and it wisped by her. German had Meg in a corner leaving nowhere for her to go. Meg's arm shielded her; she closed her eyes, waiting for German to strike.

Mariana woke up groggy from the wine and the pills, but the noise in the cabin brought her to. When she opened her eyes, she saw German wielding the machete at Meg. The silver tip of the blade flashed and reflected in the mirror when he raised it.

"Stop! Stop! What are you doing?" Mariana screamed out at him. When German heard her voice, he hesitated. He turned slowly toward Mariana, and Meg took a brief sigh of relief.

"You are the one that I came for, you bitch. This one just got in my way." German spit out his words one at a time as he moved toward Mariana. The crashing and screaming signaled Tom that Mariana was in trouble. He broke the lock when he came barreling through the door, but Tom stopped when he saw Meg. German knelt on the bed and had the knife to Mariana's neck. German's contemptuous shrieks of hopelessness told Tom that he would have killed all of them if he had the means.

"You stay where you are," he screamed at Tom. "I'll slice your meal ticket's neck."

Tom had heard enough. He charged forward and onto the bed, knocking German away from Mariana. German struggled, and they wrestled over the machete until Tom strong-armed German to the floor.

"You don't know. You don't know this evil witch. She will lie and cheat and make you do horrible things. Let me go. Let me do what I came to do."

Mariana stretched her mouth wide open until it hurt her jaw and her neck. She hadn't known German hated her so much.

Antonio entered the cabin, grabbed German, and led him out.

"Let's go. Enough of this, *Capitán!*" There was no stuttering. Antonio handcuffed German to a pipe in a locker below deck.

Tom hugged Meg, and neither said a word to Mariana, only grateful for the positive ending.

Antonio raised the anchor and drove *Moet* through the bridge into Simpson Bay and out to sea. He took advantage of the 5:00 a.m. bridge opening. He turned *Moet* southeast toward Saint Barts. It had been a long night, and Captain Antonio Blanco had decisions to make. He had a crazy man in a locker and a boss not much better. He needed to talk, and he looked to Tom, the only person he knew he could count on.

After a long while, Tom came up the stairs to the helm juggling two cups of coffee and sat next to Antonio. Antonio offered him a smoke, and this time, Tom took one.

"You have a situation, Captain. You are in charge. Mariana tried to kill herself last night, and German almost killed her this morning."

"I know, Tom. I don't know what to do."

"Meg says that Mariana's attorney is the one you need to talk to. Talk to Mariana. Tell her how you feel; she needs guidance, and maybe she'll agree. She likes you, Antonio; maybe she'll listen. What choice does she have?"

But Antonio didn't agree. "Tom, you have been very close to Mariana. Maybe you could talk to her for me. I am afraid. She is my boss."

"Yes, Antonio, she is. But if you plan to continue to be the captain of *Moet*, you need to take control. I believe you are the man for the job. You cannot be afraid. The job is yours for the taking. You just need to step up."

Tom had been too close to Mariana, and Antonio knew it. If Tom had to be the one to be the go-between, he and Meg needed to talk. He had to come clean, more for himself than for Meg.

Travel time from Sint Maarten to Saint Barts would be about an hour. It didn't leave them time for talking. Antonio had to decide what he wanted to do with German. As captain of *Moet* by maritime law, he had the final decision, not Mariana. Once Antonio turned German over to the French authorities in Saint Barts, it would be out of his control. He couldn't say what effect German's accusations would have on Mariana. Antonio made the decision to slow their speed and delay their arrival.

"Tom," Meg pleaded, "we need to contact Mariana's lawyer. He runs everything. I would be sure that Mariana would agree. Let's talk to her. After my evening alone with her, and the things she said, I believe she tried to take her life last night. She planned it. When she failed, German almost did it for her."

Antonio hesitantly stood at Mariana's cabin door. He would confront Mariana on his own. He knocked, and she opened it. What a sight. Her once-bright eyes were black from eye makeup, and her long silky hair was a tangled mess. She had been crying. She invited him in, and she turned and sat on her bed, but Antonio waited firmly in the doorway.

"No, come out to the salon; we have to talk. Ms. Mariana, I have concerns over what happened this morning." Mariana hung her head away from him.

"You know, German is in handcuffs. He is a dangerous man. Before we go into Gustavia, I am asking you to call your attorney for advice. You hired me to be the captain, and I want to do my job with integrity. Please do what I ask."

Mariana agreed. Mariana told Antonio, Tom, and Meg about the plans she already had set in motion.

"The day before yesterday, I spoke with Hymie, my attorney and confidant. He has been unhappy about my lifestyle. My daughter is also, especially since I am alone. He wants me to sell the boat and move to Mexico near her." Antonio and Tom and Meg listened.

"I don't want to do that. I love my independence, and I am too young to give up my life."

Meg waited for what she already knew came next. The things Mariana had revealed to her the day before.

"I want to clean myself up. I want to stop drinking. I want to do good in my life before it is over."

Mariana wanted to do good, to be more than a fancy lady in high-heeled pointy-toed shoes. She wanted to put the past in the past, and she wanted her future to be one of helping others like herself, who suffered like she had. Her life had almost ended that morning—and maybe Meg's too. While she knew she had driven herself to it, she didn't want her life to end that way.

The night before had mentally and physically drained everyone aboard *Moet* for a lot of different reasons. Captain Antonio had made inroads with Mariana, but he and Angeli had a baby on the way, and he worried about his job.

Tom and Meg wanted to go to Havana, get *Tori's Seacret*, and go home. But they were entangled in this mess. Tom would not walk away from Mariana or Antonio. Most importantly, Tom had to keep the promise he'd made to himself to talk to Meg.

"Meg, we have to talk about the last few weeks. Something I should tell you."

Meg pressed her finger on his lips. "Tom, you can't tell me anything about you I don't already know. I know you love me, and this has been a chapter in our life we will put behind us."

"Meg, I am not up for what Mariana wants of us. For Antonio's sake, I think the right thing to do would be to help. We can get Mariana pointed in the right direction with this yacht venture. She has money to hire the right people to take her where she wants to go with it."

He kissed her and rubbed her back, and she kissed him. He was the best kisser ever, even though she'd only kissed a few. Right then, they could have had the best sex, but they just held on to each other until they fell asleep. Bitti went round and round and round in the covers, biting and pulling them up in a small circle under her, and when she'd satisfied herself that there were no snakes in the bed, she curled up in blankets and went to sleep too.

Later that day, when Antonio pulled into the harbor in Gustavia, the authorities were waiting to take custody of German. Mariana's daughter, Elena, and Hymie and Hulia flew in the following day to talk about Mariana's rehabilitation and her future. With the help of Silvio's influence, Tom arranged to get *Tori's Seacret* released from Havana without any hitches and home to Florida.

The Caribbean summer cruising season for *Tori's Seacret* ended. When Meg and Tom pulled into their slip, their daughter, Carol, JP and his wife, and other cruising friends threw a welcome-home party. They tied streamers and balloons on the dock, and everyone celebrated their safe return. They drank French martinis and margaritas and beers in frosty mugs. Friends even toasted with shots of tequila with salt and lime. Tom and Meg had missed all their friends more than they ever realized. The group sat around a table in the cockpit and listened to Tom tell his story. And he winked at Meg when she gave him a frown, then a smile when she said, "Ok, To-mas!"

The next day, when Meg opened the mailbox, the results of her test were among the mail. She considered tearing it up and tossing it out with the junk mail, but Meg owed so much more to her mom and to his. After all, a negative result would only mean a 50 percent chance. Meg held her breath. She tucked it into her side pocket in her handbag for another day. Maybe Tom was right; maybe she didn't need to know. But at least it was her decision.

The winter boating season passed by, and *Tori's Seacret* spent most of it getting repairs. In the springtime, Tom and Meg did cruising and fishing in local Florida waters. Meg signed up for a course in big-boat handling, and Tom took Meg out to practice driving, docking, and plotting courses. He and Meg worked together, planning for the summer of 2019. Tom changed the oil and did engine maintenance. Meg loaded the boat again. In June, they were in Key West again, the launchpad for fishing boats heading to Mexico.

At 2:00 a.m., Meg was up. She walked the dog. The wide waterway was well marked—the red light on their left, the green on their right. The clear, shallow water of the reef surrounded them, but Tom's route on the GPS showed them the way. The lights from the monitors were the only lights on in the flybridge. Their somber profiles could be seen in the reflection as they watched the position indicator on the screen. Meg turned to take her last look at the fading lights of Key West. Next stop, Isla Mujeres—Woman Island—off the coast of the Yucatán.

Made in the USA
San Bernardino, CA
14 June 2020